Islamic Banking and Finance

Dr Natalie Schoon, CFA

Bank of London and The Middle East

Published January 2009 by

Spiramus Press Ltd
102 Blandford Street
London W1U 8AG
Telephone +44 20 7224 0080

www.spiramus.com

ISBN 978 1904905 11 0

British Library Cataloguing-in-Publication Data.

A catalogue record for this book is available from the British Library.

Printed by the MPG Books Group in the UK.

To Timo – who still has an unfaltering belief that I know
everything

ISLAMIC BANKING AND FINANCE

iii

Author's acknowledgements

At the risk that I inadvertently forget to mention anyone, I would like to take the opportunity to express my thanks for all their advice and support. Professors Simon Archer and Rifaat Abdel Karim for all their support during and after my PhD research at the University of Surrey and the enthusiasm for Islamic finance they have instilled in me. Neyar Malik since without the chance meeting she had with the publishers in a library in Mayfair where she was studying for her IFQ and without which I would probably never even have started. My dear friends Dr Julinda Nuri and Dr Edith Szivas for taking time to go through an earlier draft of the book and providing extensive comments. Of course special thanks go to everyone at BLME who has provided individual sections and reviewed parts of the book and especially BLME's CEO, Humphrey Percy, for his continuous support for this undertaking. And finally, to everyone I have managed to forget – trust me, it was not intentional and all your help was much appreciated.

London, 21 November 2008

Table of Contents

CONTENTS

CONTENTS

Figures

Tables

FIGURES

Foreword

I am pleased to introduce this book on Islamic Banking and Finance which is intended to provide a practitioner's view of the subject. Although the basic concepts are, of course, explained, it is not meant to be either a theoretical or academic piece of work but rather a practical overview that will hopefully interest and inform a wide range of readers.

Bank of London and The Middle East plc (BLME) was approved by the FSA in July 2007 and is now coming to the end of its first full year of operation having enjoyed a period of healthy growth which has left it well positioned with a strong balance sheet, an encouraging pipeline of transactions and experienced professional management and staff which should all contribute to helping the bank benefit from the global growth of the Islamic Finance market. However, this book is not about the promotion of BLME, but aims to share the knowledge that we have accumulated both here and in other institutions about the practical implementation of the theory and the applications of Islamic finance to both our own and our clients' requirements. Sections 8.3.1, 11.3 and 13 written by our own in house practitioners describe BLME experiences which, generalised would take valuable insights into the workings of Islamic finance in a European environment away from the reader.

I would like to take this opportunity to commend Natalie Schoon on having had the vision to plan and execute this book which will be valued by financial industry practitioners, students of Islamic banking and academics alike. Not only does this work provide a comprehensive overview of Islamic finance but it sets out the context of how modern 21st century international Islamic banking dovetails with global conventional financial markets.

Lastly, I would like to thank the publishers for the section they have provided on taxation, and of course Allan Griffiths, Abdulkhaliq Elshayyal, and Charles Peal at BLME for their own personal insights into the business areas for which they have responsibility at Bank of London and The Middle East.

Humphrey Percy
Chief Executive Officer
Bank of London and The Middle East plc
London, November 2008

1   Introduction

Although a young segment of the financial industry, Islamic finance has gone through an exceptional growth period. Over the past 10 years the industry has grown at a rate of 15 – 20% per annum. This level of growth is expected to continue for the coming years and by far exceeds the anticipated rate of growth in conventional finance. The increase in wealth resulting from the rise in oil prices and the subsequent requirements for investments in oil producing countries is a large contributor to the expansion of the Islamic finance industry. Coupled with relatively high returns, this attracts banks and investors alike. The number of fully *sharia'a* compliant banks is increasing worldwide, and *sharia'a* compliant financial products are not only offered by Islamic banks, but equally by conventional banks using different distribution channels. Although the term "conventional" is often associated with conservative and low risk, in the context of this book the term "conventional" bank is used to identify the financial institutions that have formed part of the financial infrastructure for a long time and are not specifically based on Islamic principles. As we have seen in the recent period since the end of 2007, these can by no means be labelled conservative.

The principles that form the basis of Islamic finance are old and can be traced back through time to the profit and loss sharing principles in the Code of Hammurabi in the 18th century BCE. Philosophers and theologians alike have debated the issues surrounding justness of exchange and the charging of interest.

The modern day history of Islamic finance starts in the early 1960's with a small mutual savings project in Egypt, has grown to a multibillion dollar industry in 2008 and is still going strong. Although it is too early to say whether Islamic finance will become mainstream, it certainly provides a viable alternative to other banking services.

Before going into detail of the individual transaction types, we will first look at the history of finance and economics in general and how Islamic finance fits within that framework. The prohibitions in *sharia'a* are outlined, although it has to be noted that this is an overview of the most relevant areas for finance, and other sources may have to be reviewed for further detail. A generic explanation of the most well known Islamic financial products is provided in chapter 4, followed by an overview of how these products are distributed to clients. The transaction types are divided into four main categories; partnership contracts; instruments with predictable returns; other instruments; and bond like instruments. An overview of the amended *sharia'a* standards for *sukuk* is included in this section.

Having reviewed the theoretical background of the different transaction types and how banks bring these to market, their application in retail finance, treasury, corporate finance and private equity are described in further detail. Some overlap occurs between the theoretical description in chapter 4 and the practical uses described in chapters 6 to 9 to prevent having to go back and forth between the different chapters too often. The role of the London Metal Exchange and the Metal warrants is explored in some more detail in chapter 10.

Asset management is currently attracting a lot of attention and is described in chapter 11. Asset selection, the types of funds and a practitioner's view on equity trackers versus actively managed funds is reviewed.

But there is more to Islamic banks than just the products and services they provide. Like conventional banks they inherently run risks as part of their operations. How these risks compare and differ is explored in chapter 12. Unlike conventional banks, Islamic banks have an additional body of governance, the *Sharia'a* Supervisory Board whose role it is to ensure, among others, ex-ante and ex-post compliance with *sharia'a*, as described in chapter 13. Additional regulatory issues are addressed in chapter 14 followed by taxation and capital adequacy in chapters 15 and 16 respectively. Chapter 17 provides a brief overview of bank valuation, and more importantly the valuation of an Islamic bank from an outsider's perspective. The final chapter sheds some light on what the future may have in store.

Dates in this book refer to the Gregorian (commonly termed "Christian") calendar, but we use the terms BCE (Before the Christian Era) and CE (Christian Era), rather than the overtly Christian terms BC and AD. The Islamic calendar (or *Hijri* calendar) is a purely lunar calendar, which contains 12 months that are based on the motion of the moon. This adds up to 354.36 days per year, and so the Islamic calendar is consistently shorter than a year in the Gregorian calendar. Years are counted since the *Hijra*, that is, the migration of the Prophet Mohammed and his followers to Medina in 622 CE. The year 2008 CE equates to 1429 *Hijri* or 1429 H, with their New Year having started on 10 January 2008.

2 Historic Developments

The evolution of Islamic Finance in modern history is only a small part of overall banking history and in its current form only spans a period of around 60 years. This does not imply that Islamic finance did not exist prior to the mid 1960's. Comparable to other modes of financing it has gone through periods of increased as well as diminished popularity and in addition has ceased to exist for quite some time. This chapter will look at the general history of banking as well as the way Islamic finance has evolved.

2.1 The History of Finance

The financial industry has historically always played an important role in the economy of every society. Banks mobilise funds from investors and apply them to investments in trade and business. The history of banking is long and varied, with the financial system as we know it directly descending from the Florentine bankers of the 14th – 17th century. It should therefore not come as a surprise to anyone that the word bank is derived from the Italian word *Banco* (desk or bench), which refers to the desks covered with a green table cloth used by the Florentines to conduct their transactions.

This is however not the first occurrence of banking in history. Safekeeping of valuables was for a long time a task ascribed to religious temples, even predating the invention of money. Deposits would initially have consisted of grain, but also other goods such as cattle and agricultural implements and later on precious metals such as gold, the latter typically in a form that was easy to transport such as plates or bars. There were good reasons to store valuables in temples; they would see a continuous stream of visitors which would make it difficult for any thief to go about his business unnoticed and the temples tended to be well built and were therefore considered to be secure. Perhaps even more important was the fact that they were sacred places deemed to provide additional protection against potential thieves.

Evidence exists of priests in Babylon lending money to merchants as early as the 18th century BCE, and the Code of Hammurabi[1] which is believed to be written around 1760 BCE includes laws governing banking operations in

---

[1] The Code of Hammurabi was a comprehensive set of laws, considered by many scholars to be the oldest laws established. Although the Code of Hammurabi was essentially humanitarian in its intent and orientation, it contained the "eye for an eye" theory of punishment, which is a barbarian application of the concept of making the punishment fit the crime. The Code of Hammurabi recognised such modern concepts as that of corporate responsibility. Also see: King, L.W (2004), *The code of Hammurabi*, Kessinger Publishing.

ancient Mesopotamia. Although not the first known law, it is the best preserved one. Table 1 below contains some examples of the finance laws in the code:

Law	Description
48	If any one owe a debt for a loan, and a storm prostrates the grain, or the harvest fail, or the grain does not grow for lack of water; in that year he need not give his creditor any grain, he washes his debt-tablet in water and pays no rent for this year.
49	If any one take money from a merchant, and give the merchant a field tillable for corn or sesame and order him to plant corn or sesame in the field, and to harvest the crop; if the cultivator plant corn or sesame in the field, at the harvest the corn or sesame that is in the field shall belong to the owner of the field and he shall pay corn as rent, for the money he received from the merchant, and the livelihood of the cultivator shall he give to the merchant.
50	If he give a cultivated corn-field or a cultivated sesame-field, the corn or sesame in the field shall belong to the owner of the field, and he shall return the money to the merchant as rent.
51	If he have no money to repay, then he shall pay in corn or sesame in place of the money as rent for what he received from the merchant, according to the royal tariff.
52	If the cultivator do not plant corn or sesame in the field, the debtor's contract is not weakened.
119	If any one fail to meet a claim for debt, and he sell the maid servant who has borne him children, for money, the money which the merchant has paid shall be repaid to him by the owner of the slave and she shall be freed.
121	If any one store corn in another man's house he shall pay him storage at the rate of one gur for every five ka of corn per year.

Table 1: Selected entries from the Code of Hammurabi

In addition, any compensation for loss of articles in safekeeping and the amount of rent to be paid for having the usufruct[2] of land and different species of livestock was clearly defined.

---

[2] Usufruct is the legal right to use and derive profit or benefit from property that belongs to another person. It originates from civil law, where it is a real right of limited

At the time of the Roman Empire, money lenders would conduct their transactions from long benches in the middle of enclosed courtyards. The ancient Roman money lenders merely converted any currency into the currency of Rome which was the only legal tender in the city and did not provide any further financial services.

In ancient Greece bankers did not only convert currency but also invested and banking was no longer restricted to temples. Other entities such as money changers also conducted financial transactions including loans, deposits, exchange of currency and validation of coins. Trade finance, in the form of letters of credit flourished with money lenders in one city who would, against a fee, write a credit note that could be cashed elsewhere in the country which meant that no coins needed to be carried around on their journey, nor did guards have to be hired to protect it. Interestingly enough, most of the early bankers in Greece were foreign residents, and there is little known about the individual bankers themselves, although records have been found relating to a banker called Pasion, originally a slave, who became not only the wealthiest but also the most famous Greek banker of the time.

Credit based banking spread in the Mediterranean world from the 4th century BCE. In Egypt grain has long been one of the most used forms of money in addition to precious metals. State granaries functioned as banks, and when Egypt briefly fell under Greek rule, the Government granaries were transformed into a network of grain banks with a centralised head office function in Alexandria. Payments could be effected by transfers between accounts without any physical money changing hands.

The Romans then perfected the administrative aspect of banking and introduced enhanced regulations of financial institutions in the wider sense of the word. The practice of charging and paying interest developed further and became more competitive. However, as a direct result of the Roman's preference for cash, the development of the banking system itself was limited. With the rising popularity of Christianity, additional restrictions were introduced on the banking system, mainly due to the fact that the charging and paying of interest was deemed to be immoral. With the fall of the Roman Empire, banking declined significantly in Western Europe and did not feature again until the time of the crusades from the late 11th century CE.

The Crusades, in combination with the expansion of European trade and commerce, lead to an increase in the demand for financial services. As a result

---

duration on the property of another. A lease contract, in which one party allows another to use but not own a good, is a form of transfer of the usufruct.

of people travelling into a variety of different countries, there was a significant demand for substantial amounts of physical money that needed to be changed at various points during the trip. Any service that would make it possible to transfer large sums of money without the complications of having to carry chests full of gold around and requirements for elaborate precautions against thievery was particularly in demand. Crusades were expensive and the participants often had to lend money, which was regularly done by mortgaging land and buildings. The terms were however by far more favourable to the lender than to the borrower, as a result of which the demand for mortgages deteriorated over time.

The development of international trade led directly to the requirement for a foreign exchange type contract, the first of which was recorded in 1156 in Genoa[3]. The use of these types of contracts expanded significantly, not only because of the requirements following the development of international trade, but also since profits from time differences in a foreign exchange contract were not covered by canon laws against usury.

Financial contracts of this time were largely governed by Christian beliefs which prohibited interest on the basis that it would be a sin to pay back more or less than what was borrowed. In addition, justness of price and fairness were important underlying guiding principles that applied to society as a whole and included financial services. The evolution from an interest-free to an interest-based banking system did, of course, not happen overnight, but was based on a number of factors such as the change from agrarian to commercial economies, the move towards pricing on the basis of supply and demand, decentralisation of the Church, and the recognition of money as a factor of production[4].

During the Middle Ages, until the 13th century, the Church was the largest single entity possessing significant wealth and was an important lender. However, the impact of the Church declined and as commerce flourished and generated more wealth than could be reinvested in commerce alone, it were the merchants that lent the money to finance individual and government

---

[3] Two merchant brothers borrowed 115 Genoese pounds to reimburse the bank's agents in Constantinople by paying them 460 bezants one month after their arrival in Constantinople.

[4] DiVanna, J (2008) *A cloud is a promise, fulfilment is rain*. New Horizon Jan – March 2008

consumption[5]. Initially only lending their own money, some of the merchants became merchant bankers lending both their own capital as well as capital deposited with them by others.

Whilst in most of Europe the Christian prohibition of usury was still in place, charging interest was however legalised in Valencia in 1217 and Florence in 1403. The legalisation of interest in Florence was more significant for the development of the banking industry as we know it now since the Florentine bankers, who already had a presence in a number of European countries, started to offer loans and deposits on an interest basis.

In the United Kingdom, London was the main centre of trade and hence the majority of financial transactions were executed there, mainly from the many coffee houses in the City. In 1565, The Royal Exchange was established in London to act as a centre of commerce, and some of the banking business moved there too. However, during the 17th century stockbrokers were expelled due to their rather rowdy behaviour and the buying and selling of stocks was again confined to the coffee houses.

In the early part of the 17th century Amsterdam started to grow into a major trade hub, which in turn resulted in it becoming the financial centre of the world – a position which it managed to maintain until the Industrial Revolution in the late 18th/early 19th century – and was home to the first ever recorded economic bubble, Tulip Mania. The tulip was first brought to Holland in 1593 from the Ottoman Empire, and became so popular that in 1623 a single tulip bulb could fetch as much as 1,000 florins which was equivalent to 6.7 times the average annual income. By 1636 the price had risen to unsustainable heights and the bubble burst in 1637 as a result of an absence of buyers and abundance of sellers. Tulip Mania was only the first economic bubble of its kind. Inflated asset prices have since given rise to a multitude of busts and booms, the most recent ones being the dot.com boom and the subprime crisis.

The Industrial Revolution put America and the UK firmly on the map of international finance. With this shift of emphasis, the banks in these countries gradually gained importance over time. London and New York became the major financial hubs, later on joined by Hong Kong, Tokyo and Singapore. The main financial centre in the Middle East has long been Lebanon, until the war broke out in 1982 and the banks started to move towards Bahrain and subsequently Dubai. Increasing internationalisation in trade, commerce and

---

[5] Supple, Barry *The Nature of Enterprise* in The Economic Organization of Early Modern Europe (edited by E.E. Rich and C.H. Wilson), Cambridge University Press (1977) p 423: "Commercial enterprise was more a source than a use of capital"

manufacturing applies to banks as well and was often achieved by a combination of the establishment of new branches and acquisitions. In addition, banks started to offer financial services across the whole spectrum, from retail to wholesale, with the side effect that the once-numerous small banks have now mainly merged into a few large conglomerates offering increasingly complex financial solutions. Few relatively small banks remain.

The events of 2007 and 2008, which started with the subprime crisis, which was largely considered to be an American problem, lead to unprecedented liquidity problems and resulted in the bankruptcy of Lehman Brothers[6] and the forced sale of others such as Bear Sterns in March 2008 and Merrill Lynch in September 2008.

2.2 The History of Islamic Finance

During medieval times, Middle Eastern tradesmen would engage in financial transactions on the basis of *sharia'a*, which incidentally was guided by the same principles of justness in exchange and prohibition of usury that were also applied by their European counterparts at the time. They established systems without interest which worked on a profit and loss sharing basis. These instruments catered for the financing of trade and other enterprises and worked very effectively during and after the era known as the Islamic civilisation which lasted from late 6th to early 11th century CE. Over time, Western countries started to play a more and more important role in the world economy and as a result Western or conventional financial institutions became more dominant.

As the Middle Eastern and Asian regions became important trading partners for European companies such as the Dutch East India Company, European banks started to establish branches in these countries. The finance system they introduced was typically interest-based. On a small scale, credit union and co-operative societies continued to exist but the scale of their activities was very much focussed locally on small geographical areas.

Although it was not until the mid 1980's that Islamic finance started to grow exponentially, the first financial company in recent history based on *sharia'a* principles was the Mit Ghamr savings project in 1963. This financing project worked on a co-operative basis and whoever deposited had a right to take out small loans for productive purposes. In addition, the project attracted funds to invest in projects on a profit sharing basis. The Mit Ghamr savings project was

---

[6] Lehman Brothers was officially deemed a defaulting counterparty on the 15th of September 2008.

set up to allow the local population to have access to banking services and where possible obtain a return on their money. In 1971 the project was incorporated in Nasser Social Bank. Around the same time as the Mit Ghamr savings project, financial services based on *sharia'a* were set up in Malaysia, again to cater for the generally under banked Muslim population. The earliest financial services offered in Malaysia were savings plans for the pilgrimage (*hajj*) to Mecca.

In 1975, the Islamic Development Bank (IDB) was established in Jeddah as a multilateral development bank assisting in mobilising funds for investment for projects in the member states. In the same year Dubai Islamic Bank was founded in the United Arab Emirates as the first privately established Islamic bank.

The years since 1975 have seen the establishment of many more banks and the development of the industry into a multibillion dollar market. It is no longer just small banks offering Islamic finance. These banks themselves are growing, and large conventional banks are offering Islamic finance through their "Islamic Windows". Fully *sharia'a* compliant banks and conventional banks are actively working together to offer Islamic finance, utilising some of the structuring and distribution capabilities of the larger banks. As a result, we are seeing increasingly larger transactions being structured. As of 2008, in excess of 25 organisations in the UK are offering Islamic financial services and the Financial Services Authority (FSA) has regulated seven fully *sharia'a* compliant financial institutions[7]. The UK is well on its way to achieve its goal to become the largest Islamic Financial Centre outside the Muslim world. France and The Netherlands have both also announced their intent to become the largest centres for Islamic finance, but the required changes to their tax and regulatory systems have not yet started.

The United States, originally hesitant and only allowing Islamic financial services to be offered offshore, have amended their perception and now allows Islamic financial services being offered in the USA.

---

[7] The fully Islamic institutions authorised and regulated by the UK FSA are made up of one retail bank (Islamic Bank of Britain), five wholesale banks (European Islamic Investment Bank, Bank of London and The Middle East plc, European Finance House and Gatehouse Bank), one investment manager (Dar Capital (UK)) and one insurance company (Principle Insurance Holdings).

3   Economic Principles

"The most powerful force in the universe is compound interest"
Albert Einstein

With the development of early civilisations in Mesopotamia around 3,500 BCE came the development of cities, empires and monumental buildings. A form of writing based on pictograms was developed and initially mainly used to exchange information about different crops such as the quality and quantity delivered to a temple for safe keeping and any deductions thereof. Taxes were introduced and early economic thought started to develop.

3.1   Early Economic Thought

In ancient times commercial activities were generally not public enterprises but were actively run by the rulers and other parts of the elite such as the officials of the temples and palaces. The profits did not belong to the public but were typically kept by the elite to enhance their own financial position.

The officials of temples and palaces were in any case best placed to be the main entrepreneurs of the era. Not only were they closely associated with the royals of the time, but they had good access to information regarding economic opportunities in local and distant markets which they obtained from their extensive network. Most importantly, however, they had access to the capital required to invest in trade and enterprise.

This is not to say that all entrepreneurs of the time were rulers or temple or palace officials. There is evidence of the existence of independent merchants who would act either on their own behalf or as agents for King or temple. The latter gave rise to a very early form of one of the main theories of economics, the principal-agent problem, also known as the problem of devising compensation rules that induce an agent to act in the best interest of the principal. Given the relatively low numbers of independent merchants acting as agents, however, this problem was not too prominent at the time.

As time went on and trade routes expanded, forms of trade finance developed and, as early as the 13th century BCE, the concept of trade insurance was introduced in Hitite Anatolia and Syria. Anyone killing a travelling merchant was not only obliged to pay compensation, but also to replace the goods the merchant had with him. Partnerships were set-up between neighbouring countries, trade flourished, economies developed and concepts of demand and supply and a just price became important factors.

It is from this time that four interlinked themes started to surface: private property, justice in economic exchange and usury, with money or the value thereof, linking all of these together. These have since been researched by Greek philosophers, theologians and Islamic scholars alike at different times over the past millennia. At the time, economics was not recognised as a science, but deemed to be a branch of ethics which is in turn a branch of theology. It took until the reformation and the subsequent division of religion and state for economics to become a science in its own right.

Money and Usury

During the 4thcentury BCE, Aristotle was of the opinion that money was a medium of exchange, but did not have an intrinsic value of its own since it was merely a human social invention which has no utility in itself. Following on from that, it was fairly easy to argue that "a lender of money loses nothing of worth when lending it out".

Although there is no unambiguous basis for the ban on usury in Christianity, theologians in the early centuries CE argued that the ban on usury was absolute and without exception. The basis of this argument is formed by quite a number of different verses, among which *"Upon a stranger thou mayest lend upon usury, but unto thy brother thou shalt not lend upon usury"*[8]. Although it can be interpreted in many ways, the majority of the theologians of the time preferred to argue that all men are brothers and hence the ban on usury must be absolute.

The debate on the value of money and usury preoccupied philosophers and theologians over the ages, but although clerics have been prohibited from lending at interest since the 4th century CE, the ban was not extended to the general public until the 12th century, by which time the general perception was that lending at a fixed interest rate was unholy. At the time, most lending would be for the purpose of consumption rather than production, which was deemed immoral. There was also a large social cost involved in the form of enhanced social inequality caused by compound interest. The ban on interest did not, however, end debt finance; it simply made it more complicated and resulted in the application of different structures that had the same economic effect.

The change of society away from being largely agricultural, the growth in international trade and the increasing segregation between the State and Religion, resulted in the ban on usury being revisited and by the middle of the

---

[8] Deuteronomy 23:20-21

17th century it was generally abolished throughout Western Europe. The onset of the industrial revolution, led Adam Smith to argue that capital should be seen as a factor of production just like land, labour and building and therefore has a cost or rent associated with it. He did, however, argue that the return should not be based on usury but should only reflect the risk and any opportunity cost.

Private Property

Private property and religion has long been a contentious issue. Within the Abrahamic faiths, property is typically deemed to be owned by God with man having "stewardship" and any property should be made available for public use. Although the same view is to date held by Islamic scholars, the Church turned against this in the early 5th century CE and began to accumulate significant amounts of property.

In the 13th century many theologians started to turn against the riches of the Church and started to insist on vows of poverty. On the other hand, a large number of theologians believed that private property did not have any moral implications but, to the contrary, had positive effects in stimulating economic activity and hence general welfare. This did not, however, mean all private enterprise was endorsed, and purely seeking profit for the sake of it was still considered to be a serious sin. Like capital, private property in modern economic thought is seen as one of the factors of production, and the notion of stewardship has long been abolished. In Islamic economics, the notion of stewardship still exists and property should be applied to enhance economic activity.

Justice in Economic Exchange

Is it appropriate to make a profit purely from a difference in price? How large can this difference be before it becomes unreasonable? These are the issues that are associated with the principles of justice in economic exchange. The general perception has always been that profits are acceptable as long as the entrepreneur is not motivated by pure gain and the profit (only just) covers the cost of his labour.

It is not all that simple. At the time of the Ancient Greeks, Aristotle advocated that "a just exchange ratio of goods would be where the ratio (or price) would be in proportion to the intrinsic worth of each of the goods in the transaction". This leads to the conclusion that demand and supply are not taken into consideration at all. The Romans, on the other hand, considered demand and supply to be factors in the determination of price. Their view of a just price was any price agreed between contracting parties, without any consideration for intrinsic value.

During the 12th and 13th century, Christian theologians amended their view on intrinsic worth and came to the conclusion that the intrinsic value is determined by the "usefulness" of a good to one of the contracting parties. And although usefulness is difficult, if not impossible, to determine, the result was that goods were allowed to exchange at different prices in different places and times. An additional definition stating "one should not charge for a good more than what he would be willing to pay for it himself" was added, perhaps inadvertently leading to the demand and supply mechanisms that govern modern market economies. Although this was the general view, the opposition was of the opinion that price should purely be related to the cost of production, and any prices over and above the cost were deemed to be artificially inflated. However, these price levels did exist at the time and the leap to thinking about the need for competition and immorality of monopolies was easily made.

Over time these arguments started to converge, and the just price was accepted as the natural, exchange-established price. Eventually the view that in a competitive market, buyers and sellers will not transact at a price that is not acceptable to either one of the parties, became generally accepted.

3.2 Modern Economics and Banking

> "All men, even the most stupid and unthinking, abhor fraud, perfidy, and injustice, and delight to see them punished. But few men have reflected upon the necessity of justice to the existence of society, how obvious soever that necessity may appear to be."
>
> Adam Smith - *The Theory of Moral Sentiments*, 1759

Modern economic theory starts in 1776 with Adam Smith and his epic tome *An Inquiry into the Nature and Causes of the Wealth of Nations* in which he builds further on early economic thought. Smith identifies several factors of production beyond pure labour such as land and capital. This is more or less a direct result of the Industrial Revolution which led to a shift from largely agricultural societies to societies focussed on trading and production. Capital became an important factor of production and Smith recognises that there is a cost associated with its use. At the same time, State and religion started to become more and more segregated due to which the influence of the church on the economy significantly reduced. His earlier work, *The Theory of Moral Sentiments* which emphasised ethics and fairness has generally not been given much attention. The two works combined provide a balanced view on the start of modern economics.

Smith strongly believed in the invisible hand which guides the free market and demonstrates how self-interest encourages the most efficient use of resources in a nation's economy with public welfare being a by-product. His free market concept and demand and supply theories laid the basis for current economic thinking which in addition focuses on principal-agent problems, utility functions and market efficiency governing the balances in micro and macro economics. All economics questions arise because people, companies and governments want more than they can get. Within economics, this inability to satisfy all wants is called scarcity. As a result, every entity in an economy is continuously faced with the question of utility, or on what do we spend our (limited) resources.

In modern economics, demand and supply govern the price of a good, increasing globalisation heavily impacts the price at which some goods become available and profitability guides the majority of enterprises. "Justice in economic exchange" is still a basic principle underpinning demand and supply theories. Outsourcing of services and the production of goods to low cost overseas locations is a good example of this.

Within the overall economy, banks have a specific function which is associated with the provision of financial services. For conventional banks, this translates into the provision of a financial intermediary function and to extend investment expertise to clients. Islamic banks have a similar economic function, but the implementation of the concept differs. One of the main differences is that conventional banks make their money from maturity transformation or the difference between the short term interest rates they pay and the long term interest rates they receive. In Islamic finance the charging or paying of interest is not allowed and thus results in different modes of financing. This and other prohibitions in Islamic finance are reviewed in more details in the next section. Every transaction, including financial transactions, is subject to the law of contract which is usually embedded in common law and is an important concept within *sharia'a*. Both have substantial overlapping areas which will be explored further.

3.3 Contracts and Prohibitions

The rules laid down in *sharia'a* govern every aspect of a Muslim's life, including the way they conduct their business, the criteria for valid contracts and the prohibitions. The law of contract and prohibitions are as firmly rooted in similar principles as the old philosophies regarding money, usury, private property and justice in economic exchange.

3.3.1 Law of contract

Within the framework of *sharia'a*, a contract only exists once both trading parties have agreed on all terms including the asset, price and delivery. This is similar to (English) common law which defines a contract as a legally binding agreement or a set of promises between two or more parties which could be either in writing or oral (e.g. the purchase of this book from a bookshop). All parties have voluntarily assumed liabilities with regard to each other and, although the process can be as straight forward as buying a book for the price it is offered in the shop, it can also involve further negotiations and counteroffer(s). Nevertheless, as soon as there is unconditional acceptance by all parties involved, an enforceable contract exists.

Contract – an example

My friend Juli is offering to sell me her 2007 BMW Convertible for £12,500. Although not an unreasonable price, the car is close to its next service and the tyres need to be replaced within the next 6 months. Taking these additional costs into consideration, I offer her £10,000 instead.

Given that I have made a counteroffer, we do not (yet) have a contract. Were she to accept my offer unconditionally we would enter into a contract.

The original offer is an expression of the willingness of the buyer or seller to contract on certain terms and allows the other party to accept the offer. An offer is not open indefinitely and as long as acceptance has not occurred, both parties can change their mind. An offer can be subject to a pre-agreed time limit, but even then the offer is not binding unless accompanied by a separate binding contract to keep the offer open as is. Under *sharia'a*, it was originally stated that acceptance must be conferred during the same meeting. However, increasing globalisation means that contracting parties may not be able to meet face-to-face and modern means of communication are, similar to common law, allowed.

Under common law, a contract is valid if the following elements are met:

- **Intention.** Both parties need to have the intention to enter into a contractual agreement.

- **Consideration.** The concept of consideration is the basis for courts on which to decide whether an agreement that has resulted from the exchange of offer and acceptance should be legally enforceable.

Consideration implies that there is an element of mutuality about the exchange, with something being given by each side. In the example in the box above, the considerations are the car versus the money. Within English law, consideration is described as follows:

> A valuable consideration, in the sense of the law, may consist either in some right, interest, profit or benefit accruing to the one party, or some forbearance, detriment, loss of responsibility given, suffered or undertaken by the other. (Curie vs. Misa, 1875)

The consideration has to be sufficient, but whether or not it is adequate is typically out of scope of the courts.

- **Certainty of Terms**. The terms of the contract must be clear and unambiguous. If one of the terms is not settled, the agreement is not a contract.

- **Capacity.** Parties must have the capacity to enter into a contract, which means they have to be mature and sane. Sanity can either be temporary or permanent. Temporary insanity also applies when someone is under the influence of drugs or alcohol. The notion of maturity and sanity of counterparties implicitly applies under common law as well. However, unlike common law in the Western economies where counterparties are generally considered mature once they have reached the age of 18, under *sharia'a* the legal age differs by school of thought and hence by country. On top of that, the legal age in Islamic countries often still differs between boys and girls.

- **Informed Consent.** Parties need to have entered into the agreement voluntarily and should not have been forced into the agreement.

- **Legality.** The purpose of the contract should not be illegal.

Under *sharia'a*, the elements of a contract are largely the same as the ones mentioned above. In addition however, there are a few additional conditions with regard to the asset:

- **Permissible**. The asset needs to be permissible in the eyes of *sharia'a*. This means that it should not be prohibited (*haram*) i.e. no conventional banking and insurance, alcohol, pork, gambling, adult entertainment, tobacco and defence. Illicit drugs are implicitly excluded since a contract involving an illicit drug would by its nature be illegal.

- **Ownership.** Parties need to have ownership of the asset that is involved in the transaction which implies that short selling is prohibited.

- **Ability to Deliver.** Parties need to be able to deliver. Amongst the different schools of thought, the majority of the classical schools are of the opinion that the owner needs to have physical ownership prior to being able to sell any good or property. However, a number of classical scholars and the majority of modern scholars are of the opinion that the ability to deliver can either be absolute or non-absolute. The latter is, for instance, allowed for immovable goods which will be supplied directly to the end buyer, goods in transit or in the event the seller provides direct access to the goods.

3.3.2 Contract validity

Whether it is a conventional or a *sharia'a* compliant contract, the rules regarding validity are the same. Although a *sharia'a* compliant contract has more elements that need to be satisfied, the general rule remains the same. A contract for which any of the appropriate elements is not met is void, voidable or unenforceable.

- **Void**. A contract that is void has technically never existed. Any goods or money exchanged between the parties need to be returned, even if they have been sold on to other parties.

- **Voidable**. If a contract is voidable, it operates in every respect as a valid contract unless one of the parties moves to declare the contract void. Once the contract is declared void, anything obtained under the contract must, where possible, be returned. In the event goods have been resold before this point in time, the original owner will not be in a position to reclaim them. In the event goods have been resold, the other party will have to compensate the original owner.

- **Unenforceable**. If a contract is unenforceable, it can not be enforced in the courts of law if one of the parties refuses to honour their part of the transaction. Any item dispatched under the contract can not be reclaimed by the original owner.

  A special case exists for contracts that are unenforceable until authorised. This situation occurs when an agent, dealing on behalf of a counterparty, has exceeded his authorisation and will require the ultimate counterparty to authorise the transaction. Examples of this are where a buyer offers a discounted price and the seller's agent agrees under the condition he will have to obtain authorisation from the seller, or a trader exceeding his own or the counterparty's limit.

3.3.3 Principles of Contract Applied to Financial Instruments

The elements of the law of contract mentioned in this section first and foremost apply to contracts of exchange, or trade transactions where one party purchases goods from another against payment. Financial instruments do not typically take the format of a contract of exchange, with the exception of foreign exchange contracts where the consideration does not involve any goods changing hands, but solely involves different currencies. However, this does not mean that the elements of contract do not apply to any other financial instruments.

Some of the general principles that can be applied to financial transactions are directly derived from the underlying principles of contract law.

Consciousness: Parties should consciously and willingly agree on the conditions of contract without compulsion or duress. An implication of this is that any agreement made in a state of unconsciousness (such as under the influence of intoxicants or imposed by force) is not valid.

Clarity: Parties must be aware of all the implications of the conditions laid down in a contract. Any ambiguity (except triviality) will make the agreement invalid.

Capability: Parties must be reasonably certain that they are capable of complying with all conditions of the contract. One of the implications of this is that sale of any goods (or services) which are not owned and possessed by the seller at the time of the contract is not valid.

Commitment: Parties must have the intention and commitment to respect the terms of a contract both in letter and spirit.

For Islamic financial transactions, with two exceptions, the other elements of contract such as ownership and existence of the asset also apply which results in the fact that Islamic financial transactions typically have an asset or enterprise bias.

3.4 *Sharia'a* and Prohibitions

Sharia'a, and hence also the prohibitions therein, do not just apply to Islamic finance, but govern every aspect of a Muslim's life. In commerce, following the ethics of *sharia'a* is seen as an important choice of business. The ethical framework recognises that capital has a cost associated with it and is in favour of wealth generation. However, making money with money is deemed immoral, and wealth should be generated via trade or investments.

Financial transactions are strongly based on the sharing of risk and reward between the provider of funds (the investor) and the user of funds (the entrepreneur). In addition, the credit itself is not the starting point of any transaction, but productivity is. Credit worthiness however, plays an important role in the funding decision process and collateral and other risk mitigants are widely accepted.

Sharia'a identifies three major prohibitions, each of which will be described in further detail in this section.

3.4.1 Usury

Riba is generally interpreted as the predetermined interest collected by a lender, which the lender receives over and above the principal amount it has lent out. Although a small minority of philosophers argue in favour of interest, the general opinion is that the *Quranic* ban on *riba* is absolute and without rationalisation. *Riba* comes in various guises, but two main forms are distinguished:

- Excess compensation from pre-determined interest (*riba al naseeyah*). This form of *riba* is the most basic form of interest and is the monetary compensation for an amount provided to a borrower.

- Excess compensation without consideration (*riba al fadl*). This form of *riba* occurs when the price in a sale transaction is in excess of a fair market price or, put differently, when there is inequality of the exchanged counter values.

- *Riba* does not only apply to money, but also to commodities that used to have a similar function to money i.e. gold, silver, wheat, barley, dates and salt.

The prohibition of *riba* in Islamic finance means that no interest can be charged or received, which is different from conventional finance, where interest is deemed to reflect growth, economic circumstances and the availability of capital. It is a widely accepted view that the word *riba* is derived from *raba* which is generally translated as increase. The majority of scholars conclude that *riba* is prohibited because it creates unfairness for either the lender or the borrower, or even the economy. In Egypt however interest payments are allowed for groups of the population that can not lose their capital such as orphans and widows.

Unfairness of *Riba*

Riba can be viewed as unfair from three different perspectives as outlined below.

For the borrower

Riba or interest creates unfairness for the borrower when the enterprise makes a profit which is less than the interest payment, turning his profit into a loss. Consequently, a consistent loss may result in bankruptcy and loss of unemployment while the loan and the interest still have to be paid back.

For the lender

Riba or interest creates unfairness for the lender in high inflation environments when the returns are likely to be below the rate of inflation. In addition, unfairness for the lender occurs when the net profit generated by the borrower is significantly higher than the return on capital provided to the lender.

For the economy

Riba or interest can result in inefficient allocation of available resources in the economy and may contribute to instability of the system. In an interest based economy, capital is directed to the borrower with the highest credit worthiness. In an environment where profit and loss determine the allocation of capital, the potential profitability of the project is dominant and the allocation of capital could be more efficient.

Recent research[9] is taking this line of thinking further and is looking at the severity of the punishment associated with *riba*, which implies that it is more than an economic or financial sin. Other economic crimes such as theft carry lesser punishment, which could lead to the conclusion that *riba* is associated with self generation, which is deemed to be a transgression to the divine domain and hence attracts the most severe punishment. This is in line with Thomas Aquinas (Money does not reproduce itself) and St Bonaventure (In itself and by itself money does not bear fruit but the fruit comes from elsewhere). Others argue that interest is only prohibited when it is usurious since that would result in unfairness.

---

[9] Dr Azeemuddin Subhani – PhD research McGill University Montreal, Canada. From interview in New Horizon, July – September 2008, pp. 10 – 12

3.4.2 Uncertainty and Gambling

Gharar is generally translated as uncertainty, but different schools of thought have different views on what *gharar* includes. The literal meaning of *gharar* is to unknowingly expose oneself or one's property to jeopardy and is interpreted in each of the following ways:

1. *Gharar* applies exclusively to cases of doubtfulness or uncertainty as in the case of not knowing whether something will take place or not, which for instance applies to uncertainty over the asset of the sale and can be extended to uncertainty of specifications or ownership;

2. *Gharar* only applies to the unknown, but not to cases of doubtfulness. This view is adopted when the purchaser does not know what he has bought or the seller does not know what he has sold;

3. *Gharar* applies to a combination of the above which covers both the unknown and the doubtful. "*Gharar* occurs where consequences of a contract are not known". This approach is favoured by most jurists.

Uncertainty regarding the asset, price or delivery date all cause *gharar*. In essence, *gharar* refers to acts and conditions in exchange contracts, the full implications of which are not clearly known to the parties. The prohibition of *gharar* does not relate to situations where it is not possible to reveal all details simply because it is in the nature of the asset that not all exact details are known.

Gharar – an example

Recently my friend Mirjam made an offer on a house that was built in the 1850s. The seller, who has owned the house for 10 years, informed her that there were no structural problems and no damp issues. On inspection, the surveyor found that half of the beams underpinning the floor and a large part of the wall were seriously decayed as a result of a major damp problem which, given the state of the beams, was estimated to have existed for at least five years. This is a case of *gharar* since it is reasonable to assume the seller must have known of this condition, and has deliberately withheld this information.

My friend Edith on the other hand has just bought a house built in the 1960s and has asked the seller for information regarding the foundation of the house. The seller told her that as far as he was aware it was a solid concrete foundation. Although there is uncertainty involved, this is deemed to be trivial *gharar* and is permissible. Some trust has to exist in this case between buyer and seller, as the seller is not deliberately withholding any information but is relaying the information as he knows it.

Maysir occurs when there is a possibility of total loss to one party in the contract, and is associated with games of chance or gambling. It has elements of *gharar*, but not every *gharar* is *maysir*. Anything related to uncertainties of life and business activities involving an element of chance and risk-taking are not subject to either *gharar* or *maysir*. One of the distinguishing features of Islamic finance is the sharing of risk between entrepreneurs and financiers, and hence not all types of risk taking are prohibited. The following risk types are generally defined:

- Entrepreneurial risk incurred in the normal course of business. Enterprises make profits and occasionally incur losses. Generally profits tend to outstrip any losses since otherwise no society would have any entrepreneurs at all. Willingness to take an entrepreneurial risk is not deemed to be a moral evil and Islam encourages investment. It is fulfilling a need that a society can not do without, and the risk and associated uncertainty are permissible.

- Possibility of natural disasters and calamities occurring. These risks are completely out of the control of an individual or business and are acceptable risks to take. Protection against these risks, also known as force majeure, by means of mutual insurance is permissible.

- Risks that arise from uncertainties related to activities voluntarily undertaken which are not part of everyday life and arise from types of 'games' people devise. The risks involved are unnecessary for the individual (the risk does not have to be taken) and unnecessary for society (taking the risk does not add any economic value to the wealth of the society). These risks are akin to gambling which is prohibited.

3.4.3 Impact of Prohibitions on Islamic Finance

As a result of the prohibitions in *sharia'a* the majority of conventional financial instruments are not suitable to Islamic finance in their existing form. Rather than lending money at interest, Islamic banks provide financing on a profit and loss sharing concept, and take ownership of the underlying asset. The prohibition on *gharar* and *maysir* result in the fact that forward contracts and other derivatives are not permitted. In addition short selling is prohibited since the seller needs to own the asset.

4 Islamic Finance Products Explained

Due to the prohibitions on interest, gambling, uncertainty and short selling explained in chapter 3.4, Islamic financial products are not the same as conventional financial products. Accumulation of wealth is encouraged but not by making money with money. There always has to be an underlying asset or enterprise that requires financing. Generally it can be stated that Islamic finance is in many ways similar to merchant banking, is conservative and applies solid banking principles. There are a number of products in Islamic finance, the main ones of which are explained in this chapter. This section focuses solely on the technical framework in which these transaction types work. How they can be applied in practice is elaborated on in later chapters.

4.1 Definitions

The definitions below are only associated with transaction types and parties to the transaction. A more comprehensive list is provided in the appendix. These are by no means all the terms used in Islamic finance and different words can be used to identify the same subject. In addition, due to the fact that Arabic is a phonetic language, the spelling of the same word in English in the table below represents what the word would sound like, but might be spelled different in different languages.

Word	Description
Hawala	Transfer of money from one person to another. The recipient may charge an administrative fee which should not be proportionate to the sum of money.
Ijara	Bilateral contract allowing the sale of the usufruct for a specified rent and a specified period. A lease.
Ijara wa Iqtina	Lease with transfer of ownership at the end of the lease period or finance lease. Variations exist such as the *ijara muntahia bittamleek* which is a finance lease structure in which the lessee has the option to exercise his right to purchase the asset at any time during the lease period.
Istisna	Sale with deferred delivery. Payment can be in a lump sum in advance or progressively in accordance with progress made. Delivery of good is deferred.
Kafala	Guarantee or third party obligation.

Word	Description
Mudaraba	Partnership contract. Sub-set of *musharaka*.
Mudarib	Party in a contract providing knowledge and skill.
Murabaha	Deferred payment sale or instalment credit sale.
Musharaka	Partnership contract in which all parties provide both capital and skill and expertise.
Musharik	Partner in a *musharaka* contract.
Qard	Interest free loan.
Qard al Hassan	Interest free loan. Often used in charitable context. Recipient has the moral obligation to repay the principal.
Rab al Mal	Party in a contract providing finances.
Rahn	Collateral pledged.
Salam	Sale with deferred delivery. Payment is paid in full and up front, delivery of good is deferred.
Sarf	Purchase and sale of currency. Only allowed at spot for equal value.
Sukuk	Plural of *sakk*. Represents partial ownership in assets. *Sukuk* are technically neither shares nor bonds but have characteristics of both. Profit is based on the performance of the underlying assets or projects.
Tawarruq	Purchase of a commodity that is immediately sold on to a third party (usually using the original seller as agent) on spot for cash. Form of reverse *murabaha*
Wa'd	Unilateral Promise. Undertaking or promise by one party to do or not do something in the future.
Wakala	Agency contract. Often applied to brokerage, asset management and investment activities.
Wakil	Agent in a *wakala* or agency contract.

Table 2: Selected word list

4.2 The Asset

Any Islamic financial transaction needs to be free of interest, gambling and uncertainty and in addition needs to be associated with either an asset or an enterprise. The asset of the transaction needs to fulfil a number of criteria:

Permissible

The asset needs to be permissible in the eyes of *sharia'a* which means it should not be any of the forbidden items such as conventional banking and insurance, alcohol, pork and non-compliant food production, gambling, tobacco, adult entertainment and weapons, arms and defence manufacturing.

Existence

The asset should be in existence at the time the counterparties enter into the contract. Exceptions to this criterion exist when the purpose of the contract is to grow, build or construct the underlying asset.

Ownership

The asset should be owned by the seller. This does not imply that the seller needs to have the goods with him there and then. Ownership could also be constructive. Under constructive ownership, the goods are under direct control of the owner even though he may not physically have them with him. However, selling a car that is currently owned by my brother under the assumption he will sell it to me is void. Under the same principle that one can not sell what one does not own, short selling, which is particularly popular with hedge funds, is prohibited.

Ability to deliver

The seller has to be able to deliver the goods; absolute inability to deliver the goods results in the contract being void. Non-absolute inability to deliver applies to immovable goods or where possession is constructive. For example, I have bought a crane which is currently awaiting instructions for delivery at the factory. In this case, I am the owner, have taken constructive possession and am in a position to sell. Even though I can not deliver the crane here and now, my inability to deliver is non-absolute. Either the buyer or I can, after all, instruct the factory directly with the delivery details. This also applies to goods in transit.

Specific

The subject must be specific and determined without any uncertainty. There are several ways to determine the asset, which largely depend on the type of transaction and how it is conducted. The easiest example is when you purchase something in a shop. You pick it from the shelf, and therefore the asset is as specific as it can be. Alternatively, it is possible to specify all details in a contract (e.g. the plans when buying real estate that still needs to be developed) or the distinguishing parts for mass produced goods (e.g. 100 Watt Phillips light bulb pear shaped, clear glass).

The general prohibitions, the contract elements and the restrictions on the asset do not just apply to trade; they equally apply to financial transactions. As a result, the transaction types in Islamic finance differ from conventional finance. Short selling and speculative transaction types such as futures, options and other derivatives are not permissible. In addition, the transaction always needs to be associated with an underlying asset or business. For non-Arabic speakers, an additional complexity is added with the Arabic names of the different products. On top of this, the English spelling of the names differ which is due to the fact that Arabic has a different alphabet and the language is phonetic. The remainder of this chapter deals with the different products available in Islamic finance.

4.3 Transaction Types

A variety of transaction types is available within Islamic finance to cater for a wide range of financial instruments.

The transaction types available for funding purposes can be subdivided into two main categories, profit and loss sharing partnership methods on the one hand, and transactions with a more predictable or fixed return structure such as leasing and deferred payment sales on the other hand. Partnership transactions are favoured by scholars due to the fact that they are designed to share risk and reward which is in line with Islamic economic thought. Partnership transactions require continuously close working relationships between the partners to ensure all partners are comfortable with the way the project or company is run and its profitability.

Banks and their regulators favour transactions with predictable returns which do not require significant monitoring by the bank to ensure they receive the correct profit share.

In addition to the financing type contracts, other financial instruments are available such as foreign exchange, letters of credit, agency contracts and guarantees. The remainder of this section is divided into three categories. Partnership contracts, structures with predictable returns and other contract types. *Sukuk*, or Islamic bonds, are covered in a separate section.

4.3.1 Partnership Contracts

There are two different structures for the partnership contracts, *musharaka* and *mudaraba*, with *mudaraba* being a subset of the *musharaka* contract. The main difference between the two structures is related to what the partners provide to the partnership.

4.3.1.1 Joint Venture

Musharaka means sharing, which in financial instrument terms translates to a partnership or joint venture type arrangement. In a *musharaka* all parties provide capital as well as skill and expertise to the project, and share the profits and losses. Skill and expertise could range from labour to management. Although more than two parties can be involved in the partnership, the general rule is that each and every one of the partners provides a share of capital as well as skill and expertise to the joint venture. However, it is possible for any partner to be exempted from being actively involved in the day to day operations of the partnership and become a sleeping partner that solely contributes capital. Some scholars argue that the profit share of the sleeping partner should be in strict proportion to his capital contribution. On the other hand, there are scholars that would advocate that the sleeping partner receives a lower proportion of the profit thus recognising the additional efforts from the other partners. In this case, the proportion of capital is not the only factor to be considered in determining the profit sharing ratio. The liability of the partners is technically unlimited.

Musharaka transactions are typically suitable for investments in business ventures or specific business projects, and need to consist of at least two parties, each of which is known as *musharik*.

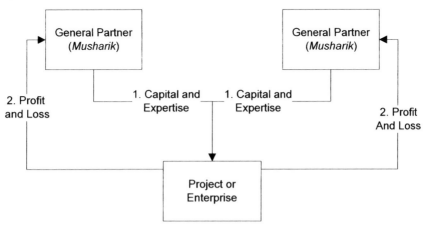

Figure 1: Simple *musharaka* transaction

Once the contract has been agreed between the partners, the process can be broken down into the following two main components:

1. **Cash and Expertise**

   All partners bring a share of the capital as well as expertise to the business or project. The partners do not have to provide equal amounts of capital or equal amounts of expertise.

2. **Profits and Losses**

   In a perfect world, the project will accrue profits which will be shared between the partners according to the ratios agreed in the original contract. To the contrary, any losses that the project might incur are distributed to the partners strictly in proportion to capital contributions. Although profits can be distributed in any proportion by mutual consent, it is not permissible to fix a lump sum profit for any single partner.

Musharaka transactions are generally for a relatively longer term and can be terminated due to liquidation, sale or one of the partners buying out the other.

Diminishing *musharaka*

The diminishing *musharaka* is a special form of a *musharaka* transaction in which it is agreed between the parties at the outset that one of the partners will, over time, purchase units in the *musharaka* venture from one of the other partners at a pre-agreed unit price. At the start of the agreement, the project is divided into a number of equal units. The repurchase agreement can be gradually over time at a fixed or increasing number of units per period. Alternatively, the repurchasing of units could be as and when it suits the purchasing party. In a diminishing *musharaka*, the repurchasing agreement is part of the contract.

As the purchasing party to the project accumulates more units, his proportionate share of the capital increases and hence his liability for any loss. Profit ratios will be revised either at each purchase or on a periodic basis depending on the agreement between the partners.

4.3.1.2   Passive Partnership

The *mudaraba* transaction is a partnership transaction in which only one of the partners contributes capital (the *rab al mal*), and the other (the *mudarib*) contributes skill and expertise. The *mudaraba* transaction type is a subset of *musharaka.* Although the investor can impose certain mutually agreed conditions in the contract, he has no right to interfere in the day to day operations of the business. Due to the fact that one of the partners is running the business and the other is solely providing capital, the relationship between the partners is founded in trust, with the investor having to rely heavily on the *mudarib*, his ability to manage the business and his honesty when it comes to profit share payments.

Mudaraba transactions are particularly suited to private equity investments or for clients depositing money with a bank and are often the underlying transaction type for the restricted and unrestricted investment accounts.

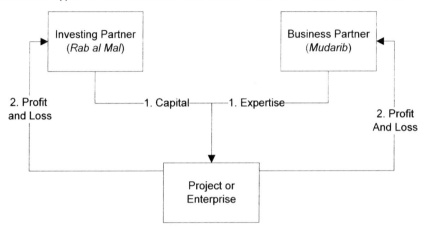

Figure 2: Simple *mudaraba* structure

Once the contract has been agreed between the partners, the process can be broken down into the following main components:

1. **Capital Injection**

   The investor, also known as *rab al mal*, provides capital to the project or company. Generally, an investor will not provide any capital unless a clearly defined business plan is presented to him. In this structure, the investor pays up 100% of the capital.

2. **Skill and Expertise**

   The *mudarib* or business manager's contribution to the partnership is his skill and expertise in the chosen industry or area.

3. **Profit and Loss**

   If all goes well, the project will accrue profits which will, similar to the *musharaka* transaction, be shared between the partners according to the ratios agreed in the original contract. Any losses are solely attributable to the investor due to the fact that he is the sole provider of all capital to the project. In the event of a loss, the business manager does not receive any compensation (*mudarib* share) for his efforts. The only exception to this is when the business manager has been negligent, in which case he becomes liable for the total loss.

Contrary to the *musharaka* in which partners have unlimited liability, the investor or *rab al mal* in a *mudaraba* transaction is only liable to the extent of the capital he has provided. As a result, the business manager or *mudarib* can not commit the business for any sum which is over and above the capital provided.

The *mudaraba* contract can usually be terminated at any time by either of the parties giving a reasonable notice. Typically, conditions governing termination are included in the contract so that any damage to the business or project is eliminated in the event that the investor would like to take his equity out of the venture.

4.3.2 Instruments with Predictable Returns

Instruments with predictable returns are typically favoured by banks and their regulators since the reliance on third party profit calculations is eliminated. There are four main instruments in this category: *murabaha, ijara, istisna* and *salam.* Some of the agency agreements (*wakala*) also provide the option for a predictable return. However, due to the fact that this is not always the case the agency agreements are not included in this section but described in further detail in section 4.3.3.6.

4.3.2.1 Deferred Payment Sale

A *murabaha* transaction is a deferred payment sale or an instalment credit sale and is mostly used for the purchase of goods for immediate delivery on deferred payment terms. In its most basic form, this transaction involves the seller and buyer of a good as can be seen in figure 3 below:

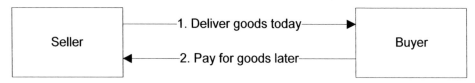

Figure 3: Simple *murabaha* structure

As part of the contract between the buyer and the seller, the price of the goods, the mark-up, the delivery date and payment date are agreed. The sale of the good is immediate, against future payment. The buyer has full knowledge of the price and quality of goods he buys. In addition, the buyer is also aware of the exact amount of mark-up he pays for the convenience of paying later. In the context of trading, the advantage to the buyer is that he can use the goods to generate a profit in his business and subsequently use the profit to repay the original seller.

The underlying asset can vary, and can include raw materials and goods for re-sale.

In Islamic finance, the *murabaha* transaction can be applied to trade finance or interbank liquidity. Further details on the application in Islamic finance can be found in Chapters 8.1 and 7.1 respectively.

4.3.2.2 Leasing

An *ijara* transaction is the Islamic equivalent of a lease and is defined as a bilateral contract allowing for the transfer of the usufruct, which basically means that one party (lessor) allows another party (lessee) to use his asset against the payment of a rental fee. Two types of leasing transactions exist, operating and finance leases. Both are called *ijara* in Arabic, but a finance lease has the addition *wa iqtina* to signify that at the end of the transaction period the ownership of the asset is transferred to the lessee. The only distinction between the two is the presence or absence of a purchase undertaking from the lessee to buy the asset at the end of the lease term. In a finance lease, this purchase undertaking is provided at the start of the contract. Under no circumstances can the lease be conditional on the purchase undertaking (i.e. the lessor can not stipulate he will only lease the asset if the lessee signs a purchase undertaking).

Not every asset is suitable for leasing. The asset needs to be tangible, non-perishable, valuable, identifiable and quantifiable.

In an operational lease, depicted in figure 4, the lessor leases the asset to the lessee, for a pre-agreed period and the lessee pays pre-agreed periodic rentals. The rental or lease payments can either be fixed for the period or floating with periodical re-fixing. The latter is usually done by linking it to a conventional index such as the London Interbank Offer Rate (LIBOR).

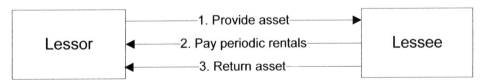

Figure 4: Operating lease

At the end of the period, the lessee can either request to extend the lease or hand the asset back to the lessor. The lessor takes a view of the residual asset value at the end of the lease term, and takes ownership risk. When the asset is returned to the lessor at the end of the period, he can either lease it to another counterparty or sell the asset in the open market. If the lessor decides to sell the asset, he may offer it to the lessee.

In a finance lease, as depicted in figure 5, the process is the same as for an operating lease, with the exception that the lessor amortises the asset over the term of the lease and at the end of the period the asset will be sold to the lessee.

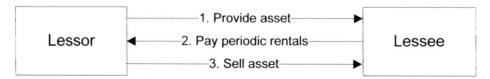

Figure 5: Finance lease

As with an operating lease, rentals can be fixed for the period or floating. As part of the lease agreement, the lessee provides the lessor with a unilateral purchase undertaking which specifies the amount at which the lessee will purchase the asset upon expiry of the lease. Three options are possible:

1. Gift. In this case, the lessor has completely amortised the asset and once all rentals are paid, there is no further payment required from the lessee to obtain the asset.

2. Against fixed payment. At the end of the lease, the lessee becomes the owner of the asset once he has paid the purchase amount agreed in the contract.

3. Against market value. At the end of the lease, the lessee becomes the owner of the asset once he has paid the market value to the lessor.

In practice, options 1 and 2 are most common.

In both forms of lease or *ijara* the lessor is the owner of the asset and incurs all risk associated with ownership. Whilst the lessee bears the responsibility for wear and tear, day-to-day maintenance and damage, the lessor is responsible for major maintenance and insurance. Due to the fact that the lessee is using the asset on a daily basis, he is often in a better position to determine maintenance requirements, and is generally appointed by the lessor as an agent to ensure all maintenance is carried out. In addition, the lessee is, in some cases, similarly appointed as agent for the lessor to insure the asset.

In the event of a total loss of the asset, the lessee is no longer obliged to pay the future periodic rentals. The lessor however has full recourse to any insurance payments.

4.3.2.3   Short Term Production Finance

A *salam* contract is a purchase contract in which payment is made now against future delivery of an asset. The *salam* contract is exempt from two of the conditions of contract that normally apply: at the time of contracting the asset does not have to be in existence, and the seller does not need to have ownership. In its simplest form, *salam* is a contract between a buyer and a seller for which payment of the full transaction amount occurs today for goods to be delivered in the future. This is depicted in Figure 6 below:

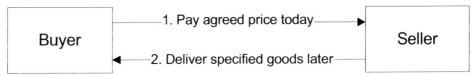

Figure 6: Simple *salam* structure

Salam contracts are typically short term (1 – 3 months), but could be entered into for longer periods. Due to the fact that the goods still need to be produced, they can only be transacted on the basis of their attributes such as type, quality and quantity but can not be attributed to an individual supplier, factory, batch or field. Any good that can not be specified by its quality and quantity (e.g. precious stones) can not be subject of a *salam* transaction. As a transaction type, it is most suitable for the financing of agriculture or small construction and manufacturing projects. The seller has a contractual obligation to deliver the specified quantity and quality at the agreed delivery date. This means that in the event that the seller has not managed to manufacture or grow the required quantity and quality, he will have to go to the open market to buy the differential and fulfil his contractual obligation. Hence the goods involved must be commodities that are freely available in the market.

The advantage to the seller lies in the fact that he will have the funds to enable him to produce the underlying asset. The buyer on the other hand obtains an asset in the future and is working on the expectation that the future price of the asset will be higher than the current price he is paying for it. The buyer takes a business risk in this transaction, and it is therefore not subject to any of the prohibitions regarding uncertainty and gambling.

4.3.2.4 Long Term Production Finance

Like a *salam* contract, an *istisna* contract is a purchase contract for future delivery of an asset, and is exempt from the same two conditions regarding the asset, ownership and existence. Unlike the *salam* contract, in an *istisna* contract, the payment to the producer or contractor of the asset does not have to be in full in advance. Payment is likely to be in various instalments in line with the progress made on the development of the asset and is therefore well suited to project finance and construction.

The asset typically needs to be manufactured, constructed or processed and is of a significant size and capital outlay. The *istisna* contract is generally longer term.

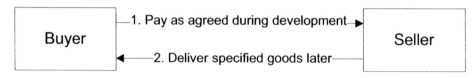

Figure 7: Simple istisna structure

Under the simple *istisna* structure depicted in figure 7, it is assumed that the buyer has sufficient funds available to pay for the asset during its construction. However, this is not necessarily the case and the seller (manufacturer) or a financier could lease the asset to the buyer for a pre-agreed period of time.

In the event a financier or bank is involved, the structure is often known as a parallel *istisna* in which the buyer commissions the financier to manufacture the specified asset for the purchase price. In parallel, the bank commissions a third party, the contractor, to manufacture the same asset for a lower price. A parallel *istisna* can be depicted as follows:

Figure 8: Simple parallel istisna structure

Like the *salam* transaction, the buyer takes a business risk in this transaction, and it is therefore not subject to any of the prohibitions regarding uncertainty and gambling. Further detail on how this structure can be applied to financing can be found in sections 8.2.2 and 8.3.2.

4.3.3 Other Instruments

Besides the profit and loss sharing instruments and the financing options with a predictable return outlined above, there are other financial structures that do not necessarily fall into either of these categories.

4.3.3.1 Contract of Exchange

A contract of exchange concerns the buying and selling of any asset between two or more parties in a single transaction. There are three forms of contracts of exchange:

1. **Goods for goods**. The exchange of one asset for another without any money changing hands. This form of trade is also known as barter trade.

2. **Goods for money**. The exchange of an asset in return for payment in money.

3. **Money for money** (*sarf*). The purchase and sale of one currency for another.

Option 1 (goods for goods) and 2 (goods for money) cover the most basic trades involving purchase and sale. Both could be conducted in a shop, over the phone, via the internet or any other medium acceptable to the parties involved. Offer and acceptance and validity requirements as outlined in section 3.3 have to be met, and the asset has to meet the eligibility criteria in section 4.2.

The money for money or foreign exchange contract is no exception, but in addition has a few other characteristics that are worth mentioning. To begin with, these contracts do not only apply to money in its current form of coins and banknotes, but also apply to include the money-like commodities of the olden days i.e. gold, silver, barley, wheat, dates and salt. In addition:

- The counter values have to be of an equal amount and have to be exchanged immediately. In a finance context, this means that FX Spot transactions are acceptable, but forward contracts are not;

- The contract of exchange should not be subject to conditional options such as "I will sell you £2,000 in return for € 2,500 if the rate moves above €1.25 per pound";

- Payment does not have to be in physical cash. Payments over account, cheques, using on-line banking etc are equally acceptable as long as the relevant account is in credit; and

- Netting of amounts in different currencies between the same parties and settling the net amount is allowed.

ISLAMIC FINANCE PRODUCTS EXPLAINED

What is not acceptable, however, is entering into a foreign exchange transaction using a credit line provided by the bank since that amounts to selling something you do not own.

4.3.3.2 Letters of Credit

Letters of Credit as an Islamic financial instrument are similar to conventional letters of credit and are an undertaking by a bank to make a payment to a named party against the presentation of the stipulated documents. Letters of credit are often used in combination with trade type transactions such as *murabaha* and *salam*, and, depending on which party requests it, provide certainty that the goods are delivered prior to payment is made or transfers the risk of non-payment to the financial institution issuing or confirming the letter of credit. Although the bank may charge an administration fee, this fee can not be proportional to the amount covered by the contract.

SITPRO, the Simpler Trade Procedures Board in the UK, which was set up in the 1970s to enhance the efficiency of international trade flows describes a letter of credit as follows[10]

> "In simple terms, a letter of credit is an undertaking by a bank to make a payment to a named Beneficiary within a specified time, against the presentation of documents which comply strictly with the terms of the letter of credit.
>
> Its main advantage is providing security to both the exporter and the importer, but the security offered however, comes at a price and must be weighed against the additional costs resulting from bank charges. The exporter must understand the conditional nature of the letter of credit and the fact that payment will not be made unless the terms of the credit are met precisely.
>
> An importer/buyer (Applicant) may open a letter of credit if they wish to ensure that the exporter/seller (Beneficiary) has performed those requirements as per the underlying sales contract, by making the documentation requested conditions of the credit. (N.B. The sales contract is not an inherent part of the letter of credit, although the letter of credit may contain a reference to such contract).
>
> When an exporter asks for payment by letter of credit, he is transferring the risk of non-payment by the buyer to the Issuing Bank -and the Confirming Bank if the letter of credit is confirmed-, providing the exporter presents the

---

[10]   Sitpro   trading   advice: http://www.sitpro.org.uk/trade/lettcredintro.pdf. International regulations for letters of credit are described in detail in Uniform Customs and Practice for Documentary Credits (UCP 600) issued by the International Chamber of Commerce.

required documents in strict compliance with the credit, with the exception of cash in advance. For the exporter a letter of credit is the most secure method of payment in international trade provided the terms of the credit are met.

The following diagram shows those involved in a letter of credit transaction:

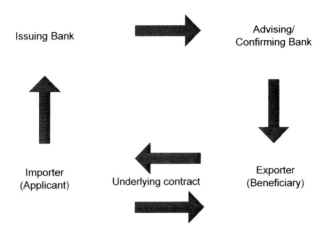

All parties in the letter of credit transaction deal with documents, not goods."

The description above applies to conventional letters of credit, but the concepts are equally valid for letters of credit based on Islamic principles. Although the last sentence in SITPRO's document specifically mentions that the parties deal with documents, not goods, there is always a physical underlying asset that is represented by the documents. Different types of letters of credit exist, such as irrevocable, confirmed and stand-by.

4.3.3.3 Guarantee

A financial guarantee is a guarantee provided by one party (the guarantor) to cover any shortfall in a third party payment. An example of a guarantee is when parents provide a guarantee to the bank for their child's payments under a home purchase plan. In the event the child misses a payment, the parents will automatically be liable.

Contrary to conventional finance, in Islamic finance, guarantees can not be used to assure profits or to guarantee business performance, but only to guarantee payment in the event of shortfall or default by a named counterparty.

In Islamic finance, the guarantor can not charge a fee for providing the guarantee.

4.3.3.4 Unilateral Promise

A *wa'd* is a unilateral promise from one party to another, and can for example be structured along the lines of "I promise to pay you £15 next week if you help me organise my brother's birthday party". Acceptance by the other party is not required, since this is not a bilateral contract. The conditionality in this phrase is also acceptable for the same reason. However, in order for this to turn into a contract the second party needs to signify his acceptance.

Bilateral promises on the same goods, for the same price, between the same counterparties and for the same future date are not accepted by the majority of scholars due to the fact that this is deemed to mimic a forward contract. An example of a bilateral promise would be when one party promises to buy €125 against £100 in 30 days and the other party promises to sell €125 against £100 on the same date. Forward contracts are prohibited since they are deemed speculative.

4.3.3.5 Down Payment

An *arbun* represents a non refundable down payment on a purchase which signifies the buyer's intent to buy the asset and is typically made toward a good that will be delivered at a later date. It is depicted in its most simplistic form in Figure 8 below.

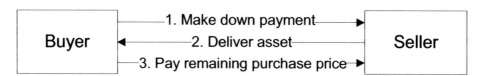

Figure 9: Simple *arbun* structure

The down payment forms part of the overall price agreed between buyer and seller, but is non-refundable in the event the buyer later decides not to take delivery of the asset. Simplified, the steps are as follows:

1. Buyer and seller agree a price and buyer makes a down payment (e.g. 20% of the purchase price). The asset is specified and the delivery date is agreed;

2. On the agreed delivery date, the seller delivers the asset to the buyer, or the buyer collects the asset from the seller;

3. On the agreed delivery date, after inspecting the asset, the buyer pays the remaining purchase price (e.g. 80% of the original purchase price).

Arbun – an example

My brother recently agreed to buy a motorbike from Biker's Best, a specialist motorbike garage, for €4,995. The motorbike is not new, and has been in the showroom for a few weeks. The seller needs to check the motorbike before it is collected and service it to ensure that it is road worthy.

Although the deal is done, the seller would like to some sort of guarantee, and does not want to be in a position where he has done all the work only to find the buyer has changed his mind. The seller requests a down payment and they agree on €995. When my brother went to collect the motorbike, he paid the remaining €4,000.

If he had pulled out of the purchase, he would have lost his €995 which the seller would have kept to cover the work he had done in making the motorbike ready for sale.

4.3.3.6 Agency Agreement

A *wakala* agreement is the agreement that governs the principal – agent relationship between two parties where one party is requesting another to act on its behalf. The application of the *wakala* agreement is varied and can range from appointing an agent (*wakil*) to purchase or sell an asset, to the investment of funds. The agent or *wakil* is entitled to a fee for his services. In addition, any profit made by him over and above a pre-agreed anticipated profit rate could be granted to him as an incentive. In Islamic finance, the agency agreement is often used to govern restricted and unrestricted investment accounts as described in section 6.3 or interbank placements as described in section 7.1.4.

4.4 Bond-Like Instruments

Sukuk is currently probably the most well known word from the Arabic language, especially in the financial world. *Sukuk* translates to legal instrument of deed and is the plural of *sakk* which means cheque. *Sukuk* are often classified as the Islamic equivalent of a bond, although there are a few differences. This section highlights the most common features of bonds and contrasts them with *sukuk*.

4.4.1 Bonds

Bonds are tradable financial instruments issued by a company, corporation or government, are typically long term and allow the holder to receive interest before the distribution of profits to the shareholders. Bonds have been around for several centuries and were popular with Kings who needed to borrow heavily to finance their war efforts. The variety of bonds is too large to describe here in detail. The main characteristics will, however, serve a purpose when comparing bonds and what is generally known as their Islamic counterpart, *sukuk.*

- **Coupon.** The coupon, which represents the interest rate payable of the bond, can be either a fixed rate for the life of the bond, or can be linked to a benchmark rate such as the London Interbank Offer Rate (LIBOR) plus a mark-up. The coupon is typically paid either annually or semi-annually.

- **Credit rating**. Any rating is primarily based on the issuer. To enhance the credit rating, and hence the chances of the holders to be repaid in the event of default, bond structures can have collateral attached to them.

- **Market.** Bonds can be bought either directly from the issuer (the primary market) or from another bond holder (the secondary market). In the secondary market the pricing of the bond is based on the view buyers and sellers have on the movement in interest rates in combination with the coupon of the bond, credit worthiness and other economic circumstances.

- **Ownership.** The holder of a bond does not have any ownership interest over the company or a specific asset and as a result do not incur any ownership risk. The bond holders have a security interest in the underlying asset.

- **Redemption.** Redemption of the nominal value of the bond is either at the due date or upon liquidation, and could be either in cash or, in the event of convertible or exchangeable bonds, in shares. In the event of default, bond holders have priority for repayment over shares.

4.4.2 Sukuk

From the view point of Islam, conventional bonds have two major draw backs and as a result are prohibited. First, they pay interest, and secondly there is generally no underlying asset. *Sukuk* are an Islamic security comparable to a conventional covered bond but are not debt instruments.

Contrary to conventional bonds, *sukuk* are normally linked to an underlying tangible asset. Intangible assets can potentially be subject to *sukuk*, and, although increasingly accepted by scholars, this is not widely accepted as a possibility. The ownership of the underlying asset is transferred to the holder of the *sukuk* certificates together with all ownership benefits and risks. This gives *sukuk* characteristics of both equity and bonds. *Sukuk* currently issued have a shorter term than conventional bonds and are typically three to five years.

The *sukuk* holder owns a proportional share of the underlying asset, and has a financial right to the revenues generated by the asset. However, as mentioned before, the holder is also subject to ownership risk, which means he is exposed to any risk and potential losses associated with the share of the underlying asset. Conventional bonds on the other hand remain part of the issuer's financial liability.

Sukuk are not a separate instrument, but are more like structures facilitating the funding of large projects which would be beyond the capability of either an individual or a small group of investors. *Sukuk* can be listed on recognised exchanges and, with the exception of the *sukuk al salam,* are tradeable. Like conventional bonds, *sukuk* can be bought from the issuer or in the secondary market. Unlike the conventional bond market, however, *sukuk* tend to be held to maturity and the secondary market is not very active. Although quotes are provided by some market makers, the spreads between bid and asking price are particularly wide and availability of issues is currently thin.

4.4.2.1 Generic Structure

At the heart of the *sukuk* structure lays a Special Purpose Vehicle (SPV) that purchases the asset from the original owner on behalf of the *sukuk* holders. The SPV is often set up as part of the group of companies selling the asset and hence raising the funds. In the interest of the *sukuk* holders, the SPV needs to be bankruptcy remote, which means that any insolvency of the original seller of the asset does not affect the SPV. In addition, the SPV should not attract any negative tax implications and will need to be established in a tax friendly jurisdiction. With the exception of *murabaha* any of the earlier mentioned partnership and predictable return structures, as well as a *wakala* can be the underlying structure for a *sukuk. Murabaha* is not applicable for securitisation since the asset has already been delivered but payment is deferred; securitising these transactions would therefore amount to debt trading. The exception to this is that in Malaysia, following the Shafi'i school of thought, regulators and market players have permitted this type of securitisation.

The generic underlying *sukuk* structure is depicted in Figure 9 below, although it should be taken into consideration that variations occur depending on the underlying transaction type.

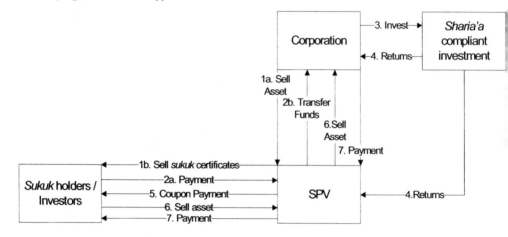

Figure 10: Generic *sukuk* structure

Although the steps differ for the different structures, the underlying principles remain the same and involve the following steps once the SPV is in place:

1. The corporation sells an asset to the SPV, which the SPV divides up in equal units of usually $1,000 or £1,000 and transfers on to the *sukuk* holders. In the event the underlying transaction is a *musharaka* or *mudaraba* the underlying asset can be represented by a share in the corporation or partnership.

2. The *sukuk* holders transfer the funds representing the number of certificates they bought to the SPV who transfers the total proceeds minus any costs to the corporation.

3. The corporation invests the funds in the *sharia'a* compliant investment stipulated in the contract.

4. The *sharia'a* compliant investment either generates profits and losses (for partnership type contracts) or pays a return (for predictable return type instruments).

5. The SPV collects profits and losses or returns and pays (typically quarterly) coupons to the *sukuk* holder.

6. At maturity, the *sukuk* holder sells the asset to the SPV, who in turn sells it back to the corporation.

7. Money flows from the corporation to the *sukuk* holders through the SPV.

Sukuk are not only issued by corporations, but also by governments and other sovereign entities and public enterprises in which case the "corporation" in the above structure can be replaced accordingly.

4.4.2.2 New AAOIFI *Sukuk* rules

Before going into more detail on the individual structures, it is worthwhile to have a brief look at the *sukuk* rules issued by the Accounting and Auditing Organisation for Islamic Financial Institutions (AAOIFI). The role of AAOIFI is described in more detail in chapter 14.1.5, and only the *sharia'a* standards for *sukuk* are included here.

From an accounting perspective, *sukuk* must be clearly defined and bankruptcy remote. In addition, any transaction in which ownership of an asset is involved requires a true sale. The only exception to this rule would be in countries where for legal or regulatory reasons it is more efficient to keep the asset on the balance sheet of the issuer of the *sukuk*.

In February 2008 the AAOIFI *sharia'a* supervisory committee refined the *sukuk* rules and incorporated the following restrictions:

- **Purchase Undertaking**. A purchase undertaking by the issuer is typically part of the structure and serves as a guarantee to the *sukuk* holders that their investment will be returned to them at the end of the period. Only in a *sukuk al ijara*, which is based on a sale and lease-back transaction, is it allowed to have a purchase undertaking at a price pre-agreed at the start of the transaction. In *sukuk al mudaraba, sukuk al musharaka* and *sukuk al wakala*, a purchase undertaking is allowed. However the price can not be agreed in advance but is the market price of the underlying partnership or asset on the maturity date.

- ***Sukuk* manager guarantee**. The *sukuk* manager can not provide a guarantee to make good the shortfall of any income to the *sukuk* holder. Due to the fact that there is no longer a guarantee in case of a default, *sukuk* will rank *pari pasu* with ordinary secured debt.

- **Reserves.** The *sukuk* manager is entitled to build up reserves out of the profit or rentals to cover any potential future shortfall, which partly offsets lack of a guarantee. However, amounts will have to be appropriated to the reserve before distributing the profit to the *sukuk* holders. This provides potential to offer different tranches which will allow investors to invest according to their risk appetite.

The tightening of the rules will result in enhanced *sharia'a* compliance of *sukuk* issued and increased transparency.

4.4.2.3 *Sukuk* Based on Partnership Transactions

Sukuk based on partnership transactions are either based on a *musharaka* or a *mudaraba* transaction. The underlying transactions work in the same way as described in paragraph 4.3.1, with the difference being that one of the partners is now the SPV instead of an individual investor.

On the maturity date, the sale of the units needs to be at market value, which will need to be established by an independent surveyor.

In both structures, the risk to the *sukuk* holder is similar:

- **Contract is making a loss.** In this case, the SPV and hence the *sukuk* holder is responsible for the loss in proportion to the capital provided. The investor is not responsible for any losses in excess of the capital provided, or for losses caused by negligence of the managing partner.

- **Managing partner can not buy the units at maturity.** This leaves the sukuk holders with the units and they do not receive their original investment back. Due to the fact that the *sukuk* holders own the shares in the project, they could instruct the SPV to find another buyer which could result in a lower sales price and will most certainly have an impact on when the investors will get their capital back.

Sukuk al musharaka

In a *sukuk al musharaka* the underlying transaction type is a partnership or *musharaka,* and both partners are a *musharik* to the transaction, although the SPV, on behalf of the *sukuk* holders typically is a sleeping partner and is not providing any skill or expertise in managing the partnership. Graphically this transaction can be depicted as follows:

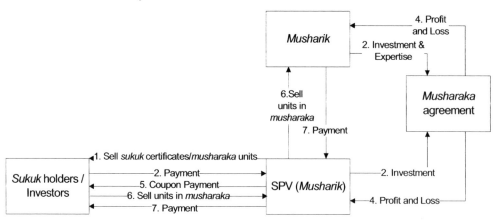

Figure 11: *Sukuk al musharaka*

Both partners invest in a project or company governed by a *musharaka* agreement. The *musharik* share of the SPV is divided in equal units and sold to the *sukuk* holders. At the end of the period, the *sukuk* holders sell the units in the partnership to the other partner.

Sukuk al mudaraba

In a *sukuk al mudaraba* the underlying transaction type is a partnership or *mudaraba* in which only one of the partners, the SPV on behalf of the *sukuk* holders, provides the capital and acts as the *rab al mal*. Graphically this transaction can be depicted as follows:

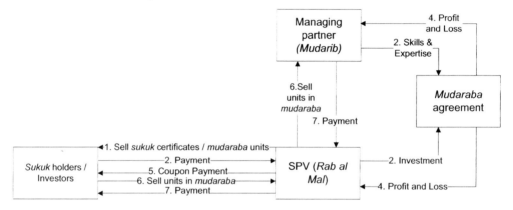

Figure 12: *Sukuk al mudaraba*

The SPV invests in a project or company governed by a *mudaraba* agreement. The investment of the SPV is divided in equal units and sold to the *sukuk* holders. At the end of the period, the *sukuk* holders sell the units in the partnership to the managing partner.

4.4.2.4   *Sukuk* Based on Predictable Return Transactions

Sukuk based on predictable return type transactions are either based on an *ijara, salam* or *istisna* transaction. The underlying transactions work in the same way as described in paragraph 4.3.2, with the difference that one of the partners is now the SPV instead of an individual investor. *Tawarruq* and *murabaha* transactions are not suitable for securitisation since that would amount to debt trading which is permitted.

Sukuk al ijara

In a *sukuk al ijara* the underlying transaction type is a lease or *ijara*, and is typically a sale and lease back structure. Generally, the funds released by the sale and lease back, will be invested by the lessee in *sharia'a* compliant projects, and can for instance be applied to expansion of the company. Graphically this transaction can be depicted as follows:

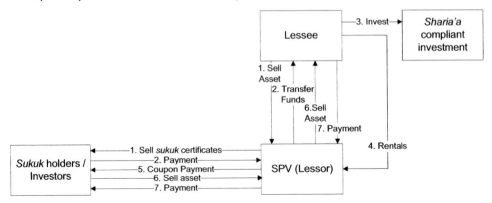

Figure 13: *Sukuk al ijara*

The lessee sells the beneficial title of an asset to the SPV under a sale and lease back agreement, and signs a purchase undertaking to buy back the asset at maturity at the same price. The SPV divides the asset in equal units and sells the beneficial ownership to the *sukuk* holders. Maintenance and insurance obligations are generally transferred to the lessee by means of an agency agreement. At the end of the period, the *sukuk* holders as lessor sell their shares of the asset back to the lessee via the SPV.

As in an *ijara* transaction, the rental can be either fixed or floating with a periodic reset based on a recognised benchmark such as LIBOR. The lessee is not necessarily dependent on the investment to ensure he can honour his rental obligations. However, the success of the investment will have an impact on the ability of the lessee to buy back the asset at the end of the period.

The risks to the *sukuk* holder are:

- **Lessee can not pay rentals.** In the event the lessee can not pay the rentals, the *sukuk* holder does not receive any coupon payment. Although it is in the interest of all parties that any default in payment will be resolved between them, the situation could occur that the lessee becomes insolvent. In this case, the *sukuk* holder has first recourse to the proceeds of the sale of the asset.

- **Asset becomes impaired.** If the asset is damaged beyond repair, the lessee is no longer responsible for the rental payments. The *sukuk* holder has full recourse to the insurance payout. However, insurance claims tend to take a long time to pay out.

- **Lessee can not buy back the asset at the end of the lease period.** Even though a purchase undertaking is in place, a situation could occur where the lessee can not buy back the asset, for instance due to insolvency. In this case, the SPV can sell the asset to another party and pay the *sukuk* holder from the proceeds of the sale. This may result in a lower sale price and hence a loss to the investors, and will most certainly have an impact on when the investors will get their capital back.

Sukuk al salam

In a *sukuk al salam* the underlying transaction type is a short term (typically 1 – 3 months with a maximum of 12 months) production finance transaction as described in section 4.3.2.3. Under this structure, the *sukuk* holder funds the seller during production and is paid out of the proceeds of the sale of the asset at the end of the period.

Graphically this transaction can be depicted as follows:

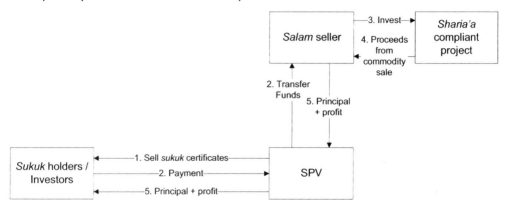

Figure 14: *Sukuk al salam*

The SPV funds a *salam* seller spot for the future delivery of a commodity. This could involve agriculture, construction or manufacturing. On the maturity date, the *salam* seller sells the commodity to the end buyer and pays the principal plus a pre-agreed mark-up to the *sukuk* holders via the SPV.

The *sukuk al salam* is similar to a zero coupon bond which pays a return higher than the original investment, but does not pay any interim coupons. Due to the underlying principles of the transaction, the asset is not transferred to the *sukuk* holder at any point in the transaction and trading the *sukuk* is not permitted as it would be akin to debt trading. The *sukuk al salam* needs to be held to maturity.

The risks to the *sukuk* holder are:

- **Commodity can not be delivered**. In the event the seller can not produce the total amount of the commodity agreed in the contract, he will technically have to obtain the commodity in the open market and deliver the same to the buyer. However, if for instance the sellers' crop fails, there is a significant probability that other's crop will have failed too and he will not be able to obtain the required quantity. In this case it will be up to the SPV on behalf of the *sukuk* holders and the seller to come to a reasonable arrangement.

- **Commodity can not be sold**. In the worst case, the seller can not sell the commodity and will not be able to redeem the *sukuk*. Technically, the *sukuk* holders could seize the asset, but will then be left with an illiquid asset. Under these circumstances the *sukuk* holder will not receive any payout.

- **Commodity can not be sold at a profit**. In this case, the commodity is sold at a price below the estimated price and the *sukuk* holder receives a smaller profit than expected, or if the price is below the production price, receives only part of his principal back.

Sukuk al salam – an example

The Central Bank of Bahrain (CBB) issues *sukuk al salam* on a monthly basis. This *sukuk* is a Bahrain Dinar (BHD) denominated debt instrument issued on a monthly basis and has a three-month (91 days) maturity. The issue amount is BHD 6 million (USD 16m)

The *sukuk al salam* is issued through a fixed-rate tender procedure where all eligible financial institutions are invited to participate. The auction procedure is executed as follows:

- Invitation letters including details on the forthcoming issue are circulated to the institutions entitled to participate in the tender.
- Tender bids are submitted to the CBB indicating the requested quantity.
- Tenders are then allotted pro rata according to quantities requested.
- Settlement of the resulting transactions takes place through debiting the participating banks' accounts with the CBB.

At the end of the period, the underlying asset (Aluminium) is delivered and sold. This results in a return which is used to pay the participating institutions their original principal plus profit.

Sukuk al istisna

In a *sukuk al istisna* the underlying transaction type is a long term production or construction finance transaction or *istisna*. The asset is usually a fixed asset such as plant or machinery and is built exactly to the buyer's specification. Due to the significant capital outlay associated with these types of transactions, the *istisna* contract is often directly followed by a finance lease. Both components of the transaction are combined in the *sukuk al istisna*.

Graphically this transaction can be depicted as follows:

Figure 15: *Sukuk al istisna*

The specification and cost of the asset are agreed between the buyer and the manufacturer under an *istisna* contract. The funds from the *sukuk* holders are transferred to the buyer in full on the issue date, but only paid to the manufacturer in accordance with the schedule agreed in the contract. Once the funds have transferred to the buyer (steps 1 and 2 in the above figure), the following steps take place:

3. The buyer manages the relationship with the manufacturer as agent on behalf of the SPV and pays the manufacturer as agreed in the contract.

4. During the manufacturing process, the SPV and the buyer have a forward rental agreement under which the ultimate buyer pays a forward rental fee.

5. The physical asset is delivered to the buyer; the beneficial title will be delivered to the SPV.

6. Once the asset has been delivered, the forward lease ceases to exist and is replaced by a lease agreement in which the ultimate buyer is the lessee and the SPV the lessor. The lessee provides a purchase undertaking and pays rentals to the SPV.

7. At maturity, the SPV sells the asset to the lessee on behalf of the *sukuk* holders.

8. The lessee pays the full settlement amount to the SPV who repays the *sukuk* holders for their initial investment.

The risks to the *sukuk* holder are:

- **Asset not delivered by manufacturer.** If the asset is not delivered by the manufacturer, the forward lease agreement ceases to exist. The buyer will negotiate the next steps, on behalf of the SPV and the *sukuk* holders. In the event the manufacturer has become insolvent, a claim for monies paid has to be made with the administrator. In any other situation, any funds paid to the manufacturer will have to be reclaimed. Non-delivery of the asset is likely to have an impact on the length of the forward lease, or may result in the transaction folding altogether.

- **Lessee can not pay rentals.** In the event the lessee can not pay the rentals for either the lease or the forward lease, the *sukuk* holder does not receive any coupon payment. Although it is in the interest of all parties that any default in payment will be resolved between them, the situation could occur that the lessee becomes insolvent. In this case, the *sukuk* holder has first recourse to the proceeds of the sale of the asset.

- **Asset becomes impaired.** If the asset is damaged beyond repair, the lessee is no longer responsible for the rental payments. The *sukuk* holder however, has full recourse to the insurance payout not withstanding that any insurance claims tend to take a long time to pay out.

- **Lessee can not buy back the asset.** Even though a purchase undertaking is in place, a situation could occur where the lessee can not buy back the asset, for instance due to insolvency. In this case, the SPV can sell the asset to another party and pay the *sukuk* holder from the proceeds of the sale. This may result in a lower sale price and hence a loss to the investors, and will most certainly have an impact on when the investors will get their capital back.

5   Distribution of Islamic Products

Islamic financial products are not only offered by banks that are fully *sharia'a* compliant – commonly known as Islamic Banks – but also by conventional banks deploying specific distribution channels. The question that arises is whether this makes a difference. One of the questions that is often raised is whether or not Islamic financial instruments offered by Islamic banks are better than those offered by conventional banks. Although there are differences in the offering, this does not necessarily make either of them better or worse. In the end, each offering will need to be reviewed on its own merit. This chapter outlines the differences in distribution channels and how Islamic and conventional banks can work together to provide the best possible financing solutions for their clients.

5.1   Distribution Channels and *Sharia'a* Compliance

In order for a financial product to be *sharia'a* compliant it needs to satisfy, at a minimum, the criteria of *sharia'a* regarding the avoidance of *riba*, *maysir* and *gharar*. Once these are satisfied and the bank obtains *Sharia'a* Supervisory Board (SSB) approval, the product or structure can be marketed as *sharia'a* compliant. As far as conventional banks are concerned, this is where *sharia'a* compliance stops. It does not for example prevent the bank from employing non-Islamically raised funds to invest in Islamic structures. Conventional banks go to market with these products via the following distribution channels:

Window – The term window is used for conventional banks carrying out Islamic financial activities and delivering them via the same distribution channels, such as branches, they also use to distribute conventional financial products. Operations and accounting, however, are segregated from the conventional operations. Examples of this in the UK are Lloyds TSB and HSBC Amanah.

Branch – The branch structure is similar to windows, but uses separate branches instead of the conventional branch network to distribute Islamic financial products. A combination of branches and windows can be used by the same bank. HSBC Amanah for instance provides Islamic financial products via their conventional branch network, but also provides these services via dedicated branches.

Subsidiary – A subsidiary is a separate legal entity that manages its own strategy within the parent's overall guidelines. Subsidiaries typically prepare separate annual reports, which are reported on a consolidated basis into the parent's annual report and accounts. An example of a subsidiary is Citi Islamic

Investment Bank which was incorporated in Bahrain in 1996, in response to US regulations which stated that American banks are allowed to offer Islamic financial services, but only via off-shore entities.

A fully *sharia'a* compliant or *sharia'a* based bank takes compliance with *sharia'a* a step further. Not only do individual products have to meet all the requirements, but all operations within the bank are required to be compliant with *sharia'a* as well. This extends to contracts with suppliers, rental contracts and labour contracts. The bank is completely set up to work in line with the ethical framework of *sharia'a*. Therefore, it is more likely to be able to structure all products to meet *sharia'a* requirements. Moreover, there is no co-mingling of conventional and Islamic raised funds since all funds are raised in line with *sharia'a* requirements.

5.2 *Sharia'a* Compliant versus *Sharia'a* Based

It is the personal preference of any investor, depositor, *sukuk* issuer or other client of a bank as to what they would consider to be an appropriate level of *sharia'a* compliance. Other factors anyone will need to consider are size, reputation and historic track record of the bank. In the end, a large conventional bank with a proven track record may generally provide a relatively higher degree of comfort than a newly established Islamic bank, although current market conditions may lead to a different view on this issue. In addition, large conventional banks have the advantage of the backing of a big balance sheet and structuring capabilities that, at least at the moment, are beyond the potential of Islamic banks. This becomes immediately clear when comparing the total assets of the largest Islamic banks with total assets of the largest conventional banks. As of March 2007, the largest Islamic bank (Bank Meli Iran) had total assets of $34 billion closely followed by Al Rajhi bank with total assets of $33.4 billion at the end of December 2007. In contrast, the largest conventional bank by total assets at the end of 2007 was Royal Bank of Scotland with assets nearing $4 trillion, followed by Deutsche Bank, BNP Paribas, Barclays, HSBC, Credit Agricole, Citigroup and UBS, all with assets in excess of $2 trillion each at the end of December 2007[11]. Even allowing for the deterioration in balance sheets as a result of the credit crunch, conventional banks are significantly larger than Islamic banks. Their large balance sheet allows them to underwrite large *sukuk* issues and to structure sizeable project finance structures, something that Islamic banks are not yet able to do. On the other hand, conventional banks provide Islamic finance as part of a broader range of financial products and although the individual offerings are *sharia'a*

---

[11] The Banker, Top 1000 World Banks, July 2008

compliant and the distribution channel is different from other financial products, a conventional bank is likely to co-mingle funds raised in an Islamic manner with conventionally raised funds. Conventional banks can also hedge positions using innovative financial products which are often not allowed in Islamic banks, due to the speculative nature of most hedging products.

A small, relatively young Islamic bank does not have a long track record and may therefore be deemed by investors and depositors to carry a higher risk. Although some comfort can be found in the fact that the bank is regulated, this is not a unique feature of an Islamic bank. Small, newly established conventional banks encounter the same issue. As a result of the smaller balance sheet size, Islamic banks are, at the moment, not in a position to underwrite large Islamic finance transactions unless they are part of a syndication effort, and even then some transactions are out of their scope due to large exposure regulations and size limitations. A *sharia'a* based bank, however, operates completely within the remit of the ethical framework defined by *sharia'a*, something that should be of significant interest to Muslims. A fully Islamic bank will not only be audited by the internal and external auditors, but will also be subjected to a review by the SSB in its capacity as an independent third party to ensure on-going *sharia'a* compliance for the whole of their business, and not just for individual transactions. This should also go a long way to counteract any reservations about dealing with Islamic banks from the perspective of investors and borrowers. An Islamic window or branch of a conventional bank likely goes through this type of ex-post compliance audit as well, but does not have to report the results in their annual report.

5.3 Competition or Opportunity

The years since 1975 have seen the establishment of many more banks and the development of the industry into a multibillion dollar market. It is no longer just small banks offering Islamic finance. These banks themselves are growing, and large conventional banks are offering Islamic finance through their "Islamic Windows", each with their own advantages.

- **Balance sheet size and structuring capabilities**. The large balance sheet size of a conventional bank and their extensive structuring capabilities can be deployed to back large Islamic financial transactions.

- **Proven track record.** Conventional banks have been around for a long time and have build up a proven track record which generally provides a relatively higher degree of certainty than a newly established Islamic bank. However, given the current market turmoil in which banks have announced large losses and are rescued by their respective governments, a long established bank is no longer likely to have this advantage over a newly incorporated entity.

- **Specialised knowledge and expertise**. Islamic banks operate completely within the ethical framework of *sharia'a* and offer skill and expertise in structuring *sharia'a* compliant instruments which conventional banks not necessarily posses.

The two types of players are very complementary, and by working closely together, they can achieve high market penetration and work on reaching the full potential of the market. Fully *sharia'a* compliant banks and conventional banks are actively working together to offer Islamic finance, utilising some of the structuring and distribution capabilities of the large banks, in combination with the specific expertise the Islamic banks bring to the table.

6 Application of Islamic Products in Retail Finance

Retail financial services for Islamic banks are typically offered in the same way as conventional banks. Islamic banks have banking halls, ATMs and offer debit cards, credit cards and cheque books with current accounts. Modern means of banking such as telephone and on-line banking and text messaging services are also considered to be part of the package.

Retail clients are not only those who are served by the banks that are referred to as high street banks in the United Kingdom, but equally encompass high net worth individuals who have requirements for similar types of products.

6.1 Current Accounts

One of the basic banking requirements for retail and corporate clients alike is the current account which allows a client to receive and pay funds, and is usually the entry point to a banking relationship. Although the total offering varies from bank to bank and from country to country, current accounts tend to be accompanied by additional facilities such as debit cards, credit cards and cheque books as well as on-line and telephone banking facilities and other features of modern current accounts.

In Islamic finance, current accounts are mainly offered using either of the following structures:

6.1.1 Qard Al Hassan

The *qard al Hassan* is an interest free loan, historically provided for charitable purposes. Often the *qard al Hassan* is intended to assist with matters such as the payment of school fees, weddings or the purchase of land to build a home. The loan has a charitable intention, but even though the recipient does not have to pay a return on the funds, he is morally obliged to repay the principal in full. The provider of the loan is not compensated for inflation.

When applied to current accounts, the client is lending funds to the bank without any requirement for interest or any other form of return. The bank is under all circumstances morally required to repay the capital, but whilst the funds are held by the bank, they can be freely invested to fund any of the bank's day-to-day operations.

6.1.2 Amanah or Wadia

The words *amanah* and *wadia* literally translate to trust, and in the context of finance it is deemed to represent safe keeping. When a bank accepts money in trust for the client these funds can not be co-mingled with other deposits or the banks own capital and can not be used by the bank to apply to their day to day operations. The bank may request the client for authorisation to use the funds in their day to day operations, but can only do so if the client expressly approves this. *Amanah* and *wadia* are closely related to the original duties of safe keeping temples and early bankers used to provide. Due to the fact that the sole purpose is safe keeping, the bank has the moral obligation to repay the capital under all circumstances, even if the client authorises the bank to use the funds.

General

Both types of account have an implicit obligation for the recipient of the funds to guarantee the capital is paid back in full, but without any further compensation.

Overdrafts are generally not allowed, but in the event a client accidentally goes overdrawn, the bank may charge an administration fee which is equivalent to the operational cost of remedying this situation. A penalty in proportion to the size of the overdraft may not be charged.

Historically, the *qard al Hassan* has been a popular tool for current accounts and still is in the Middle East and Europe. In Asia however, the *amanah* or *wadia* instruments are rising in popularity which is probably due to the fact that the *qard al Hassan* is originally associated with charitable purposes which is contrary to the purpose of a current account.

In most countries banks are legally required to guarantee deposits for conventional as well as Islamic current accounts.

6.2 Credit card

Credit cards are currently probably one of the most popular methods of payment when it comes to consumer transactions. From an Islamic finance perspective, credit cards generally have one major drawback in that they charge interest on the outstanding balance. Although clients could rely solely on debit cards and cash, this does not give them the flexibility of the payment options associated with a credit card. In addition, a credit card is widely accepted, especially when it comes to on-line payments, and provides a level of security against bankruptcy of the supplier prior to delivery of the goods or services.

Different types of Islamic credit cards are offered in the market, typically around the following structures:

1. **Periodic Service Charge**. In this structure, the card issuer charges the card holder a monthly or annual charge which is generally a fixed fee per period. Additional charges can be included for instance when the card issuer allows the client to carry forward a credit balance.

2. **Deferred payment sale**. In this structure, the card issuer allows the customer to use his card to pay for a good or service under a *murabaha* type transaction. The sequence of events is as follows:

   a. Client uses card to pay for good or service;
   b. Card issuer becomes owner of the good or service, and takes responsibility for the payment to the merchant;
   c. Card issuer immediately sells the good or service on to the client at the original purchase price plus a mark-up for payment at the end of the period; and
   d. Client pays the original purchase price + mark-up to the card issuer at the agreed future date.

3. **Lease purchase agreement**. In this structure, the card provider is the owner of the asset until the card holder makes the final payment. The client can be charged a rental fee.

4. **Pre paid credit card**. In this structure, the client deposits an amount of money on their card and uses the card to pay for goods and services. Due to the nature of the card the client can not pay for goods in excess of their debit balance and credit balances do not occur. Hence any interest type charges are easily avoided. The card issuer can invest the excess balances to generate a return as long as the investments are *sharia'a* compliant.

Variations on these structures are available and include for instance loyalty programmes.

Contrary to conventional credit cards, where the card issuer charges interest on any outstanding balance, Islamic credit cards do not attract any interest. In addition, the card issuer can not charge the client a penalty for late payment although an administration fee may be charged to cover any costs involved with recovering the debt. In the event the card issuer charges a penalty in excess of their costs, the difference will be donated to charity.

Islamic credit card issuers often require collateral such as cash deposits to reduce their exposure, and share any profits from the investment of these amounts with the client.

Islamic credit cards can typically not be used to purchase any non *sharia'a* compliant items.

6.3 Deposit Accounts

Unlike current accounts, where clients do not necessarily expect a return, savings or deposit accounts, do offer a return on capital. Deposit accounts are typically offered as an investment account, which are governed by *wakala*, *mudaraba* or *murabaha* type contracts between the bank and the client.

When applying *wakala* or *mudaraba* transactions, the depositor is the *rab al mal* and the bank is either the *wakil* or *mudarib* depending on the type of transaction. Graphically these structures can be depicted as follows:

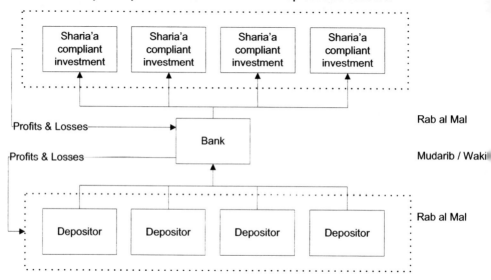

Figure 16: Two tier *mudaraba* or *wakala* structure for savings accounts

In the first part of the contract, the depositors are the investors or *rab al mal* providing capital to the bank, who is acting as the *wakil* or *mudarib* providing expertise as investment managers. The bank's responsibility is to identify appropriate *sharia'a* compliant investments which provide the maximum returns given the appropriate risk level. The relationship between the depositor and the bank takes the form of either a restricted or an unrestricted investment account.

The top part of figure 16 above governs the relationship between the bank and the clients to which it provides financing. The bank pools assets from the individual depositors with their own funds and invests in *sharia'a* compliant assets. The transactions the bank invests in vary between retail banks, which mainly fund retail clients for personal finance or home finance, and investment banks, who invest in projects, property, leases, trade finance and treasury transactions.

6.3.1 Restricted and Unrestricted Investment Accounts

Deposit accounts are typically offered to clients either as a restricted investment account or an unrestricted investment account. In both cases, the bank can co-mingle the funds from different account holders with their own funds, in which case the bank is both the *mudarib* and the *rab al mal*, and invest in a range of investment opportunities.

Under a restricted investment account, the client restricts the range of assets the bank can invest their money in. Technically the restrictions could be anything that is agreed between the bank and the client as long as the transaction is *sharia'a* compliant. In practice however, the bank will not allow a large variety in their restrictions, with a typical restriction being based on the length of time the investment is held. It is, however, not unheard of to have restrictions in place regarding the type of transaction (e.g. only leasing) or industry (e.g. no telecommunications). The type of restricted investment account that is most appropriate for an individual client depends on their investment profile, which includes time horizon, liquidity requirement and risk appetite.

For unrestricted investment accounts, the client authorises the bank to invest their money in anything the bank deems to be a suitable investment, as long as it is *sharia'a* compliant. The investment decisions are made entirely by the bank.

When governed by a *mudaraba* agreement, the bank is paid a *mudarib* share for its investment skill and expertise which is determined based on gross income minus expenses incurred. The remaining profit share is distributed to investors pro rata depending on the capital provided. In the event the bank has also invested its own funds, the bank collects a profit share on behalf of the shareholders. The *mudarib* share in combination with any profit on the banks own funds are an operational profit for the bank and are distributed to shareholders in the form of dividend or retained in the bank for future development.

In the event of a loss, the bank does not receive a *mudarib* share, and all losses are passed on to depositors in proportion to the funds provided. In the event the bank is negligent however, the loss is completely for the account of the bank.

6.3.2 Capital Certainty and Capital Adequacy

Restricted and unrestricted investment accounts are most commonly governed by a *mudaraba* or *wakala* contract, which implies that profits are shared between the bank and the depositors on the basis of a contractually agreed profit ratio, and losses are distributed in accordance with the proportion of capital provided. The capital of investment account holders is hence not guaranteed, although commercial and, in some cases, regulatory and legal pressures effectively mean that banks do anything possible to avoid passing on a loss to depositors, or not paying them a reasonable return. Different situations occur:

- **Malaysia.** Banks have a legal obligation to repay the capital and provide a reasonable return.

- **Bahrain and other Gulf Co-operation Countries (GCC).** Capital guarantees and steady returns are not a legal requirement, but are deemed to be a commercial responsibility of the bank by the regulating bodies. Regulations are in place to ensure adequate monitoring and mitigation techniques to avoid any loss of capital.

- **United Kingdom.** In the United Kingdom, banks are allowed to pass on any loss to their account holders, but only after the bank has announced the loss, and the account holder has expressly confirmed his desire to bear the loss for religious reasons.

From the perspective of the Islamic Financial Services Board (IFSB), a bank has no obligation to keep the capital intact and hence banks are not required to hold any capital to cover any eventualities associated with restricted and unrestricted investment accounts. Not all regulators however follow the same line of thought, and take the commercial risk associated with loss of capital into account when determining the capital adequacy treatments. Bahrain for example applies a capital adequacy ratio of 12% instead of the Basel II requirement of 8%. Malaysia and the United Kingdom, on the other hand, apply a capital adequacy ratio of 8%, but consider restricted and unrestricted investment accounts to have the same characteristics as conventional savings accounts.

Capital adequacy for Islamic banks is described in more detail in chapter 16.

6.3.3 Accounting Treatment

Comparing the annual reports of different Islamic banks, it becomes obvious that there is a large difference in how investment accounts are reported on the balance sheet. Although AAOIFI has created standards to enhance the transparency surrounding this, the AAOIFI standards are not mandatory in every country. The following three main reporting treatments are observed in the market:

1. **Equity.** Due to the fact that investment account holders can lose all their money, their investment has similar characteristics to the investment of a shareholder with the exception of the fact that contrary to a share, the balance in the investment account can not be sold in an open market. On the other hand, investment account holders can, within the terms and conditions of the agreement, withdraw their funds and take their business elsewhere.

2. **Off Balance Sheet.** Treating investment accounts as off-balance sheet instruments can be justified on the basis that the bank manages the funds on the client's behalf, but all losses are due to the client. This treatment is particularly suitable for fund management activities.

3. **Liability.** Treating investment accounts as a liability is justified in countries where Islamic banks can not pass any loss on to depositors and the investment account behaves like a conventional deposit or savings account. This treatment applies regardless of whether the prohibition to pass on any losses to investment account holders is incorporated in the law or deemed to be a regulatory or commercial issue.

In addition, a combination of any of the above reporting treatments is found in different bank's balance sheets. Some banks for instance, report restricted investment accounts as a combination of liabilities and off balance sheet instruments and unrestricted investment accounts as equity. However, it needs to be noted that with the development of the industry and the accounting standards, transparency on the reporting guidelines has increased.

In the UK, where Islamic financial institutions have to follow the International Financial Reporting Standards (IFRS), investment accounts are treated similarly to conventional deposit accounts.

6.3.4 Reserves

Prior to the introduction of the AAOIFI standard in 2001 to regulate profit smoothing, banks often used to apply hidden reserves in order to smooth the profits paid to unrestricted investment account holders in line with market expectations. The AAOIFI standard was not introduced to eliminate the profit smoothing practice, but rather to make the process more transparent. It is in the banks' interest to avoid any losses for investment account holders, at the same time paying account holders a profit share which is in line with their expectations. Prior to the introduction of the AAOIFI profit smoothing standard, banks typically varied the mudarib share to allow for this. Under the new standard which was introduced in 2001, banks appropriate part of the profits attributable to unrestricted investment account holders to two different reserves:

1. **Profit Equalisation Reserve (PER).** The bank appropriates funds to the PER from the profit distributable to unrestricted investment account holders and shareholders prior to the distribution of profits between the bank in its capacity to provide investment expertise and the depositors and investors. The PER has a shareholder portion and an unrestricted investment account holder portion and is used at the bank's discretion to pay a return to unrestricted investment account holders and shareholders in years when income is low.

2. **Investment Risk Reserve (IRR).** The bank appropriates funds to the IRR from the share of profit allocated to unrestricted investment account holders after the bank has taken its *mudarib* share. Amounts are released to unrestricted investment account holders at the banks' discretion to cover any losses incurred.

Although the reserves are created to cover losses and ensure profitability to investment account holders, the reserves are not owned by them, and when an unrestricted investment account holder leaves the bank, the bank will pay his account balance, but not a part of the PER or IRR. Both reserves remain with the bank.

6.4 Funds

Within Islamic finance, funds are typically offered under a *mudaraba* or *wakala* agreement between the client and the fund manager, similar to restricted and unrestricted investment accounts as can be seen in Figure 17:

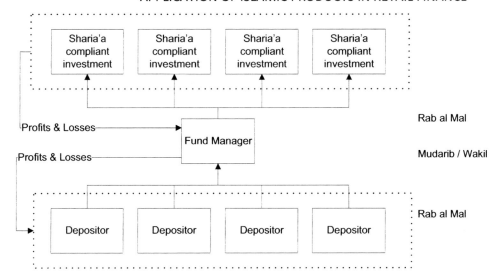

Figure 17: Two tier *mudaraba* or *wakala* structure for fund management

Although most funds currently available in the market require a minimum investment amount of $100,000 or more, the growth of the Islamic finance market makes it possible to also start offering funds with a smaller minimum capital. Investors have the opportunity to invest in index tracking funds or equity strategies for a minimum investment of £500, $500, or any denomination and minimum amount offered depending on the fund.

6.5 Mortgage Products

Islamic mortgage products, or home purchase plans as they are sometimes referred to, are generally based on either one of the following structures:

1. **Diminishing *musharaka*.** In this structure, the client and the bank jointly purchase the property. The client pays a periodic rental for the use of the part of property he does not own, which can be either a fixed rate for the duration of the contract or based on a floating rate. The part of the property owned by the bank is divided into equal units which are gradually sold to the client over time. The purchase of units by the ultimate home owner is governed by the agreement and can be monthly, quarterly or as and when it suits the ultimate buyer. The responsibility for maintenance and insurance is passed on to the end buyer under an agency agreement.

2. **Lease.** In this case, the bank buys the property and leases it to the client. Any maintenance and insurance issues are passed on to the client under an agency agreement. The rental payments can either be fixed for the duration of the lease or can be reviewed periodically. Typically the lease

amount includes a progressively increasing payment towards the value of the property, which will be 100% owned by the client at the end of the lease.

3.   *Murabaha.* In this structure, the bank buys the property and sells it on deferred payment basis to client. In some countries this can be a solution to overcome the common issue of double stamp duty. In the Netherlands for instance, the rule is that if a property is sold within six months after the original purchase, there is no requirement for stamp duty land tax on the second sale. In the United Kingdom on the other hand, any property sale attracts stamp duty land tax, even when it is sold on after a short period. There are two draw backs to this structure which are inherent to the characteristics of the *murabaha* transaction. First, it can not be extended unless there is full movement of funds i.e. the client would have to repay the full amount to the bank prior to any new facility being extended. Secondly, although the mark up can be paid in instalments, the amount is fixed for the agreed period.

4.   **Diminishing *musharaka* combined with lease.** In this structure the diminishing *musharaka* governs the transfer of the ownership from the bank to the ultimate buyer. The client leases the part of the property he does not yet own from the bank against a fixed or floating rental payment. Although a rental fee can be incorporated in a diminishing *musharaka,* and it is possible to have a repayment portion in the periodical lease payments, there might be regulatory or tax issues that would lead to the necessity to specifically combine a diminishing *musharaka* and a lease.

The diminishing musharaka and lease structures can be extended beyond the original life time of the transaction without the (remaining) principal being repaid in full. Unlimited early repayments are permitted under each of the above transactions, and late payments attract an administration fee, but this is only to cover the actual cost and can not be in proportion to the outstanding amount of the transaction.

The Financial Services Authority in the United Kingdom recognises two types of home purchase plans, being the diminishing musharaka and the lease structure[12]. Specific amendments have been made in the UK Finance Act in order to ensure there is no double stamp duty land tax associated with these transactions.

---

[12] For more information see:
http://www.moneymadeclear.fsa.gov.uk/pdfs/home_purchase_plans.pdf

6.6 Personal Loans

Generally Islamic banks prohibit overdrafts, but permit personal loans as long as there is an associated asset that is financed. Like conventional finance, both secured and unsecured personal loans are offered and the mark-up will depend on the client's credit rating as well as any collateral pledged. The main difference between Islamic and conventional personal loans is the fact that the transaction is based around an asset of which the bank has some form of ownership during the transaction.

6.6.1 Secured Personal Loans

A secured personal loan is a loan which directly finances the asset the client wants to acquire. The bank typically has ownership of the asset during the transaction and keeps the asset as collateral to protect against any negative impact of default. The most common forms of secured personal finance are:

- **Lease or hire purchase contracts.** In lease and hire purchase contracts the client identifies the asset and all its specifications and requests the bank to purchase the asset. The client then leases the asset from the bank and pays an agreed rental for an agreed period of time. The lease contract typically includes a repayment and a rental fee, and once all payments have been made at the end of the period, the asset belongs to the client. The bank has no specific expertise regarding the asset and often requests the client to act as agent to order the asset from the supplier. As can be seen from

- **Figure 18** below, the seller delivers the asset to the bank who will lease it to buyer. In practice, the asset is typically delivered directly to the end-buyer, but the legal title to the asset is delivered to the bank.

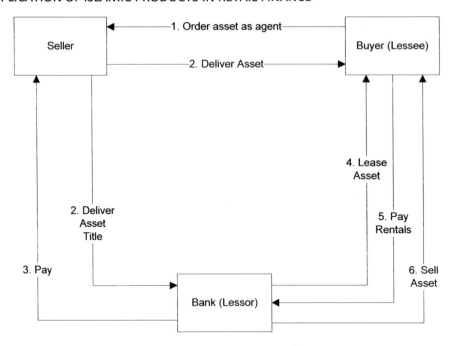

Figure 18: Lease for personal finance

- ***Murabaha* or deferred payment sales**. In a deferred payment sale, the client identifies the assets and all its specifications and requests the bank to purchase it. The bank subsequently sells the asset on to the client on a deferred payment basis. The asset, the original purchase price, the mark up for deferred payment and the payment date are all agreed in the contract. The bank has no specific expertise regarding the asset and often requests the client to act as agent to order the asset from the supplier. As can be seen from Figure 19 below, the seller delivers the asset to the bank who will sell it on a deferred payment basis to the buyer. In practice, the asset will be delivered directly to the end-buyer, but legal ownership is with the bank until the end of the lease period.

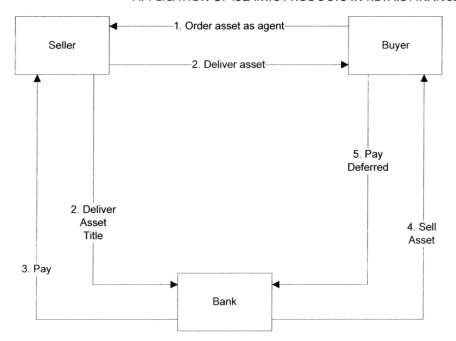

Figure 19: *Murabaha* for personal finance

Example – *Murabaha* for personal finance

Al Rajhi bank, one of the largest Islamic banks, is the owner of a number of car dealerships throughout the Kingdom of Saudi Arabia. In the event a client wants to finance the purchase of a car, the bank first assesses the amount of finance it is willing to provide. The client is then informed of the maximum amount he can spend on a car in one of the showrooms, the mark up for deferred payment and the repayment criteria.

6.6.2 Unsecured Personal Loans

Unsecured personal loans are provided to clients when they require cash which is not necessarily associated with a particular asset to be financed. The client could for instance require an amount of cash to pay for school fees or to pay for building works to be done to his home. Although collateral may be requested, unsecured personal finance is typically of higher risk to the bank due to the absence of an underlying associated asset. Unsecured personal loans are generally provided on the basis of commodity *murabaha*, which is graphically depicted in Figure 20 below.

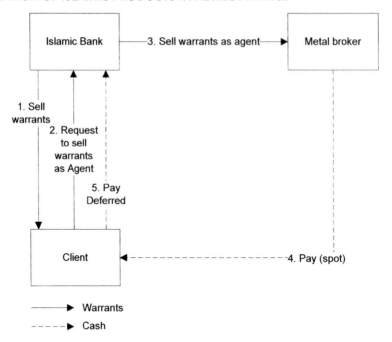

Figure 20: Commodity *murabaha* for personal finance

Although there are a variety of approaches available, the transaction flow outlined in the above graph is fairly common. Due to the fact that the client is unlikely to have a relationship with a metals broker, the bank is likely to act as an agent on behalf of the client to sell the commodities and facilitate receipt of funds into the clients account. In order to avoid any price risk, the purchase and sale of the commodity by the client take place on the same day. The end result of this is that the client has an amount of money into his account which needs to be repaid on a pre-agreed date in the future with a pre-agreed mark up.

6.7 Transfers

Transfers can be made for a variety of reasons including the payment of bills, to give someone money, or to transfer amounts to and from a deposit account. Transfers can be between two accounts held by the same person, or held by different people or organisations.

The majority of transfers will be in the same currency, but there are circumstances in which a transfer from an account in one currency to an account in a different currency is required, for instance, when paying a bill in a different country. When transferring in a foreign currency, it is permissible to request the bank to transfer an amount of money in one currency to be paid to another person in a different currency. The bank will in this case take care of the exchange of one currency to another, and this type of transaction is a combination of a currency exchange and a transfer of money, and the bank may charge an admin fee. The fee should only be charged to cover the admin expenses incurred by the bank and should not be in proportion to the amount transferred.

Paying a bill in a different currency – an example

Every now and then I transfer money to my brother in The Netherlands to pay for materials he needs to redecorate my house in Holland. Given that I am based in the United Kingdom, my accounts are all in British Pounds (GBP). My brother's accounts however, are in Euro. When I transfer money, I instruct my bank to transfer from my GBP account to my brothers Euro account without me having to first exchange from GBP to Euro and then transfer.

Let's assume I have to pay my brother 1,000 Euro:

1. I instruct my bank to transfer 1,000 Euro to my brothers account from my GBP account

2. The bank transfers the 1,000 Euro and debits my account with the equivalent GBP account

3. My bank charges me a fee of GBP 25.00

4. My brother's bank charges him a fee for receipt of funds originated from a foreign country of 25.00 Euro

---

Transferring money has not always been the responsibility of banks, but used to be done by *hawala* brokers. Under the *hawala* system, someone goes to a broker in a particular city and gives him money to be transferred to a person in a different city or country. The *hawala* broker will request another broker in the city of the recipient to make the payment, typically less a small commission. The payment instruction is normally accompanied by a request for a password, a particular document or any other proof required to identify the recipient. The first broker promises the second broker to settle with him at a later date, which is similar to the promissory notes in conventional finance. Strong evidence exists that the *hawala* system has been around since at least medieval times, but potentially a lot longer.

The *hawala* system has by no means died out and is still extensively used by migrant workers. In 2006 the International Monetary Fund estimated that $100 billion in transfers per year is not transacted via the regular banking system and an unknown part of this figure is transferred using the *hawala* system. In its current form, *hawala* brokers often keep an office in the back of a shop or a community centre, and they often import from or export to the same countries as the ones they transfer money to. A common way to settle the differences therefore is by paying inflated invoices for goods received. The *hawala* banking system works perfectly for migrant labourers with families in very remote areas of the world who are, in addition, often confused by the banking system native problem compounded by the language barrier. The main problem is that the *hawala* brokers are not regulated in the same way as other banks and financial institutions and as such form a large risk for the financial infrastructure, and they are a tempting target for those with less honourable intentions. This has, for example, become evident in the investigations into funding of terrorism activities.

7 Application of Islamic Products in Treasury

The treasury function, also known as markets division, of a bank is responsible for funding the other divisions, managing the bank's mismatch and liquidity risks, and for making markets to customers in Foreign Exchange and *sukuk*. In addition, this division of the bank assists clients in managing their money market and foreign exchange exposures using a variety of *sharia'a* compliant contracts.

7.1 Interbank Liquidity

The commodity *murabaha* is the instrument most commonly used by Islamic financial institutions to provide short term interbank liquidity.

A commodity *murabaha* is, like the basic *murabaha* transaction, a deferred payment sale or instalment credit sale and uses a commodity, usually a base metal, as the underlying asset for the transaction. In its most basic form, this transaction involves two banks, one as the buyer of a commodity and one as the seller as can be seen in

Figure 21 below:

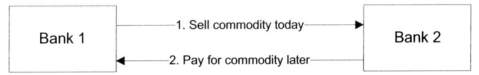

Figure 21: Simple commodity *mudaraba* structure

As in the *murabaha* transaction detailed in chapter 4.3.2.1, the price of the commodity, the mark-up, the delivery date and repayment date are agreed up front. The intention of this transaction is to replicate conventional money market transactions (i.e. the interbank market), and the banks do not typically hold the underlying commodity nor have a requirement for it. The metals are purchased and sold solely to facilitate interbank liquidity in accordance with *sharia'a* principles.

Two types of commodity *murabaha* transactions occur, deposit given and deposit taken, each of which are reviewed in more detail in the sections below. Due to the fact that commodity *murabaha* transactions are fixed rate, they are typically short term with a maximum term of one year. In addition to commodity *murabaha*, interbank liquidity is sometimes provided using a *tawarruq* transaction. All these transaction types are executed using a commodity as the underlying asset.

The criteria for commodity to be considered suitable are that it should be non-perishable, freely available and can be uniquely identified. Any commodities that were originally used as a means of exchange or money –i.e. gold, silver, barley, dates, wheat and salt – are not acceptable. The majority of commodity *murabaha* and *tawarruq* transactions use LME base metals as an asset since they meet all criteria for a commodity and are easily identifiable via warrants.

In comparison to conventional deposits, commodity *murabaha* and *tawarruq* transactions attract an additional cost associated with the purchase and sale of the warrants which could be dependent on volume and contract size. For longer dated contracts, this is not necessarily an issue as the additional cost is spread over a longer period. It does however significantly increase the price of shorter dated deposits.

7.1.1 Deposit Given

The aim of the commodity murabaha is for the Islamic bank to provide a deposit to their counterparty to generate a return. The process flow is as follows:

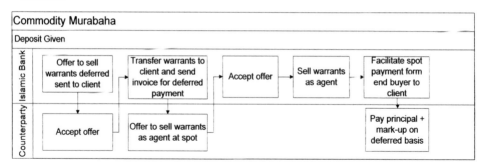

Figure 22: Commodity *murabaha* - deposit given

In this structure, the following actions take place:

1. **Counterparty buys warrants from Islamic bank.** The counterparty accepts the offer from the Islamic bank to purchase warrants on a deferred payment basis, where the mark up and the repayment date are pre-agreed.

2. **Ownership of warrants transfers to counterparty.** The counterparty is now the owner of the warrants but does not make a payment until a later date.

3. **Counterparty requests Islamic bank to sell warrants on its behalf.** The Islamic bank now acts as an agent to sell the warrants at spot to another buyer. Alternatively, the counterparty could sell the warrants in the open market. Ownership of the warrants transfers to the end buyer.

4. **Payment from end buyer to counterparty.** Whether the counterparty requests the Islamic bank to sell the warrants on their behalf or arrange to sell to a third party themselves, the counterparty will be paid the spot counter value of the warrants.

5. **Payment from counterparty to Islamic bank.** This payment takes place at a pre-agreed time in the future and consists of the principal of the original purchase plus a pre-agreed mark up.

The net result of the above movements of warrants and cash is that the counterparty now holds an amount of money against an offsetting payment to the Islamic bank for a pre-agreed principal plus a mark up at a pre-agreed future date thus creating a synthetic deposit.

It is important to note that each of the steps has to take place in the correct sequence and that the ownership of the warrants will have to transfer from one party to the next before the next action can take place.

The flow of cash and warrants in a commodity *murabaha* is as follows:

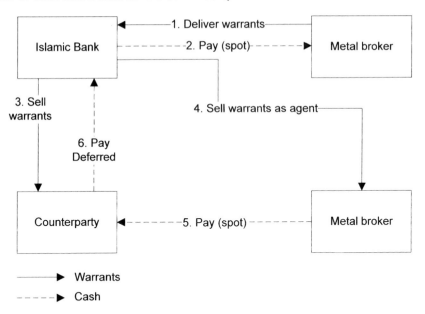

Figure 23: Commodity *murabaha*, cash and warrant flow

In steps 1 – 3 the Islamic Bank buys the warrants as a principal and subsequently sells them to the client on a deferred payment basis. The client now owns the warrants and requests the Islamic bank to act as an agent on his behalf to sell the warrants in the spot market. The Islamic bank arranges for the sale to a metal broker resulting in a synthetic interbank deposit placed by the Islamic bank with the client.

7.1.2 Deposit Taken

The aim of a reverse commodity *murabaha* is for the Islamic bank to take a deposit from the client and to repay it at a pre-agreed time including a mark up. The process flow is as follows:

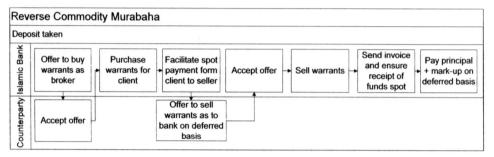

Figure 24: Reverse Commodity *murabaha* - deposit taken

In this structure, the following actions take place:

1. **Islamic bank buys warrants as agent on behalf of counterparty.** The counterparty accepts the offer from the Islamic bank to purchase warrants on their behalf.

2. **Ownership of warrants transfers to counterparty from the current owner via the Islamic bank.** The counterparty is now the owner of the warrants and pays for them at spot.

3. **Counterparty offers to sell warrants to the Islamic bank.** The counterparty is now the owner of the warrants and offers to sell them to the Islamic bank against deferred payment. Ownership of the warrants transfers to the Islamic bank.

4. **Islamic bank sells warrants to end buyer against spot payment.** The Islamic bank sells the warrants to an end buyer and receives the counter value at spot.

5. **Payment from Islamic bank to counterparty.** This payment takes place at a pre-agreed time in the future and consists of the principal of the original purchase plus a pre-agreed mark up.

The net result of the above movements of warrants and cash is that the Islamic bank now holds an amount of money against an offsetting payment to the counterparty for a pre-agreed principal plus mark up at a pre-agreed future date thus creating a synthetic deposit taken by the Islamic bank.

As with deposit given, it is important to note that each of the steps has to take place in the correct sequence and that the ownership of the warrants will have to transfer from one party to the next before the next action can take place.

The flow of cash and warrants in a reverse commodity *murabaha* is as follows:

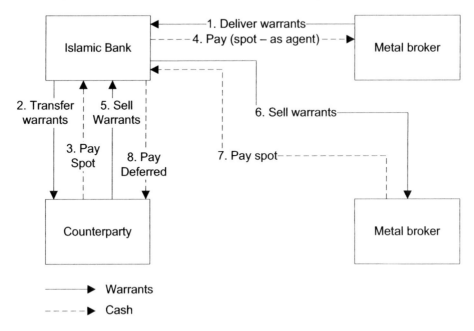

Figure 25: Reverse Commodity *murabaha*, cash and warrant flow

In steps 1 – 4 the Islamic Bank is acting as an agent on behalf of the client. The client now owns the warrants and sells them to the Islamic bank on a principal to principal basis, against a deferred payment of the principal plus a mark-up. The Islamic bank, as the owner of the warrants, subsequently sells them to a metal broker against spot payment resulting in a synthetic interbank deposit placed by the client with the Islamic bank.

7.1.3 Variation on Commodity *Murabaha*

Like commodity *murabaha, tawarruq* is a commodity based transaction for interbank liquidity purposes. The *tawarruq* has, however, some *sharia'a* issues associated with it. The main *sharia'a* issue with *tawarruq* transactions is related to the fact that the intention behind the purchase of the commodity is not to own and use the commodity. Instead, the commodity is sold instantaneously in order to obtain the required funds. Historically, although the minority of the schools of thought in Islamic jurisprudence have rejected the *tawarruq* for that reason, the majority have approved it subject to certain conditions such as an auditable ownership transfer of the commodity and separation of the purchase and sale arrangements.

Some banks that are using *tawarruq* structures have, however, not adhered to these conditions, for example by combining the sale and purchase into one single transaction in which the bank buys from, and sells to the same broker as an agent on behalf of the client. Due to the fact that sale, purchase and appointing the bank as agent are all happening in one schedule, it is almost impossible to see who owns the commodity at any point during the execution of the transaction.

Despite the differences of opinion among scholars, the *sharia'a* council of AAOIFI has approved *tawarruq* and has issued a separate standard to regulate this instrument to ensure that it is *sharia'a* compliant. Although *tawarruq* may not be the most perfect instrument and has serious *sharia'a* issues associated with it, it does serve a purpose when Value Added Tax (VAT), stamp duty or other taxation rules pose limitations on Islamic finance and the *tawarruq* is more often than not the only feasible transaction type available.

Graphically, the *tawarruq* can be depicted as follows:

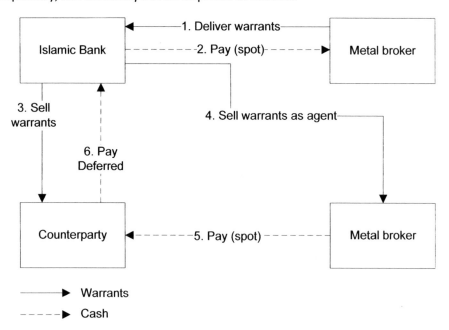

Figure 26: *Tawarruq*

Contrary to the commodity *murabaha,* in which each of the steps has to take place in the correct sequence, and ownership of the warrants will have to transfer from one party to the next before the next action can take place, in a *tawarruq* there is only one agreement in which both parties agree that the Islamic bank will sell the warrants to the client and simultaneously sells them on behalf of the client to a metal broker. Consequently, if the transaction falls through at any point, ownership of the asset is not clear.

7.1.4 Agency Contract

Between Islamic banks, interbank liquidity can be managed using a *wakala* or agency contract. Under a *wakala* agreement a bank places funds with another bank for them to invest in suitable *sharia'a* compliant projects. The structure is similar to the investment accounts for retail products and fund management structures and can be depicted as follows:

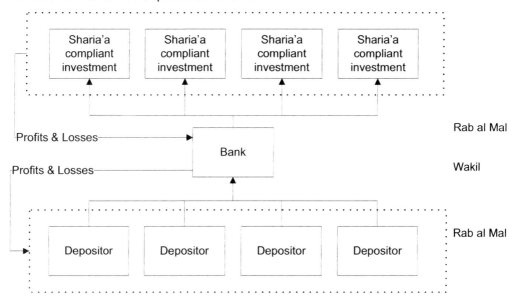

Figure 27: Two tier *wakala* structure for liquidity management

The *sharia'a* compliant investments in the figure above can be any financing the bank undertakes and can for instance include commodity *murabaha, sukuk* and leasing. The *wakala* contract is a trust contract whereby money can be placed with an Islamic institution which then pays a return based on the assets on its balance sheet. *Wakala* contracts are more restricted in their application than commodity *murabaha* transactions, since they can only be offered to other Islamic Financial Institutions whose assets are all *sharia'a* compliant.

7.2 Hedging

Like conventional banks, Islamic banks manage their risks carefully and do not leave themselves open to unnecessary exposures. Several structures can be applied to mitigate or hedge risks, the most common of which are described in this section.

7.2.1 Derivatives

The prohibitions regarding gambling and uncertainty means that options, futures and other derivatives are not generally accepted by Islamic scholars. Even forward foreign exchange contracts are generally not permitted, since they include an element of uncertainty and are priced by reflecting an interest differential. Derivatives, with their inherent uncertainty and speculative characteristics, are not acceptable in the *sharia'a* framework, but this does not mean that Islamic investors do not have any possibility of hedging their exposures. On the contrary, within the *sharia'a* framework taking measures to mitigate risk is seen as good stewardship, and hence promoted.

In the absence of options, futures and other derivatives, other contracts need to be applied, and there are two main basic contracts available to the Islamic investor to hedge against risks that occur within the normal course of their business. First, there is the *arbun* contract which is outlined in section 4.3.3.5 and is a down payment on a sales contract. In this case, the buyer and seller agree a price and date and a down payment is made. If the buyer pulls out of the transaction, he loses his deposit. If the buyer takes delivery of the asset, the down payment becomes part of the total price and only the difference is payable. This is different from an option premium which represents an amount separate from the actual exercise price.

A second type of contract that can be used for hedging purposes is the *salam* contract. This is a contract executed with spot payment in full for the purchase of assets. This can only apply to assets promised for future delivery which have commodity-like characteristics and must be fungible, such as base metals. The *salam* contract has characteristics of a conventional futures contract but, unlike a conventional futures contract, a *salam* contract must be physically settled by the delivery of the asset at the end of the contract.

Both the *arbun* and the *salam* contracts can, in combination with other available products, provide a considerable level of risk mitigation. However, the complex derivative instruments available to the conventional investors are, at this point in time, far out of reach for the Islamic investor.

7.2.2 Option to Buy or Sell

The down payment or *arbun* as described in section 4.3.3.5 can be applied to finance to achieve a result similar to a conventional option. The down payment has some characteristics of an option and provides the right to buy an asset at a price agreed today, a right which is secured by the down payment. Similar to an option, if the buyer does not purchase the asset at the agreed date, he loses the down payment. Unlike an option however, if the buyer purchases the asset at the agreed date, he only pays the difference between the agreed price and the down payment.

Like any other form of contract, the seller needs to have ownership of the asset and the asset needs to be in existence. In a financial context, the bank could for instance make a down payment on equity or *sukuk* in the secondary market.

Down Payment – An Example

Bank of London and The Middle East plc (BLME) has an equity stake in a *sharia'a* compliant company which it would like to sell and has identified a potential buyer who would like to purchase the shares in one month's time at a price agreed today. The following are the details of the transaction:

- Current share price: £2.50
- BLME's expected share price in one month: £3.00
- Client is willing to agree a price of: £3.20

The client is making a down payment of £0.20 per share in order to purchase the shares in one month's time at a price of £3.20. After one month, the following scenario's can occur:

1. Share price rises to £3.20 or above. In this case, the client will pay an additional £3.00 per share to BLME (£3.20 - £0.20) and becomes the owner of the shares;
2. Share price after one month is below £3.20. In this case, the client will not purchase the shares and lose his £0.20 per share.

7.2.3 Foreign Exchange Requirements

One of the forms of a contract of exchange is the foreign exchange contract in which one currency is exchanged for another. Within Islamic finance, exchanging one currency for another is permissible when both parties take immediate possession of equal amounts of the counter values. The contract should not be subject to any conditional options. The contract, also known as *sarf,* is a binding obligation between the counterparties to buy or sell a specified amount of foreign currency at an agreed spot exchange rate.

The stipulation of "immediate possession" implies that only spot trading is allowed, which includes not only the exchange of the amounts in physical cash, but also transfers, debiting and crediting a customer account in the different currencies or the presentation of any cheque.

Due to the prohibitions on gambling and uncertainty, forward contracts are generally not allowed since forward contracts are associated with speculative trading and the pricing includes an interest component. However, discussions are going on amongst scholars, and quite a few are of the opinion that forward foreign exchange transactions should be permitted as a risk mitigating tool for companies having a genuine business requirement to cover forward currency exposure.

Forward foreign exchange as a risk mitigating tool – an example

My Bike is based in the United Kingdom and imports bicycles from The Netherlands to sell in the UK market. My Bike receives monthly invoices from the exporter in Euro which need to be paid within 30 days. Based on experience, My Bike can estimate their payments in Euro for the next 3 – 6 months with reasonable accuracy.

On the other hand, My Bike sells the bicycles in British Pounds (GBP) and all other expenses such as rent and staff cost are in GBP.

My Bike would like to cover their exposure to Euros which occurs in the normal course of business, which is by no means speculative since they are after all in the business of selling bikes, not managing currency exposures.

7.2.3.1 Currency Swaps

An exchange of deposits can be applied to satisfy any liquidity requirement in a particular currency while at the same time placing excess liquidity in another currency with another bank. Both deposits are placed on either a commodity *murabaha* or a *wakala* basis at a profit rate of 0%. Any profit margin as well as exchange rate expectations are included in the calculations of the amounts.

The amounts are exchanged at the start of the contract and repaid in full at maturity, and the transaction can, in its simplest form, be depicted as follows:

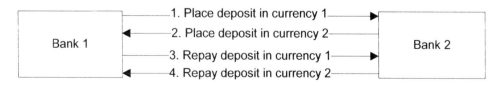

Figure 28: Exchange of Deposit

Although the exchange of deposit satisfies a requirement with regards to the availability of currencies, because of the inclusion of the forward differential the two amounts can vary widely and do not represent equal counter values at the current exchange rate. This structure can be improved upon by combining two commodity *murabaha* transactions with a spot foreign exchange transaction, or by two commodity *murabaha* transactions at a normal profit rate.

7.2.4 Profit Rate Swap

A profit rate swap is entered into by a bank in order to transform a fixed rate income stream to a floating rate income stream or vice versa. Any surplus floating rate exposure (either paying or receiving) can be transferred to a fixed rate exposure using a combination of fixed and floating *murabaha* contracts. The bank typically wants to engage in this type of structure to create certainty between incoming and outgoing profit streams. These discrepancies occur in the normal course of business as a result of the banks investments.

Two structures are typically observed in the market, both combining a series of commodity *murabaha* transactions with a promise (*wa'd*). Although the promise is legally not binding, the likelihood of either of the counterparties not honouring their promise is deemed low due to the significant commercial risk associated with breaking a promise. The two structures can briefly be described as follows:

1. At the start of the contract, counterparties enter into one long term and one short term commodity *murabaha*. The counterparty that places the short term commodity *murabaha* provides a *wa'd* to enter into all the subsequent short term transactions, until such a time that the maturity date of the long term commodity *murabaha* is matched.

2. Counterparties promise to enter into a sequence of periodic commodity transactions where the mark-up is defined based on the Swap Fixed Rate for one leg and a floating rate for the other leg. The Swap Fixed Rate is agreed for the duration of the transaction. For the floating rate leg, the mark-up over a benchmark rate (e.g. cost of funds) is agreed.

Profit Rate Swap – An example

Bank A has an outgoing fixed rate profit payment obligation of 7.5% for one year and an incoming profit stream benchmarked to, for instance, 3 month LIBOR + a mark-up of 2.5%.

Looking at the first structure, a profit swap can be achieved using one *murabaha* transaction for the total term of the transactions and a series of

---

shorter term *murabaha* transactions with the same counterparty for the same amount effectively replicating a floating profit rate. The individual shorter dated *murabaha* transactions require full movement of funds.

Graphically, this structure looks as follows assuming the cash flows in and out on the floating transactions will be netted.

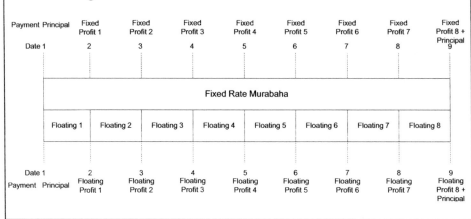

The Profit Rate Swap is beneficial for both counterparties for the duration of the transaction. However, in the event of early termination, either one of the parties could be unfairly disadvantaged as a result of the loss of commercial benefits of the transaction. This element of unfairness, which is naturally built into the contract, can be resolved in the contract between parties.

7.2.5 Selling an Asset Forward

As described in section 4.3.2.3, a *salam* contract is a structure in which an asset that is not yet in existence and not yet owned is sold against a current price for delivery at a forward date. Some Islamic financial institutions have obtained approval from their *sharia'a* supervisory board to apply a *salam* structure to sell equities forward.

7.3 Combination of Transaction Types

As can be seen from some of the transaction types described earlier, combinations of transaction types are possible. The Profit Rate Swap, for instance, combines different *murabaha* transactions and a *wa'd*, a foreign exchange solution could be structured using a spot foreign exchange transaction with one or more commodity *murabaha* transactions. The combinations are theoretically unlimited, as long as it is being taken into consideration that even though the different transaction types are wrapped up in a single structure, none of the contract elements are conditional upon each other, which would not comply with *sharia'a* principles.

7.4 Asset-Based Securities

As described in section 4.4.2, *sukuk* are created by the establishment of an SPV which is set up to acquire an underlying asset or group of assets. The SPV then issues certificates which represent participation rights in the cash flows generated by the assets for a defined period. Since they pay regular coupons, *sukuk* are generally regarded as the equivalents in Islamic Finance of Fixed Income securities in the conventional market. The role of a treasury division is to assist customers wanting to invest in *sukuk* and those who would like to raise financing by issuing *sukuk.*

Market making in *sukuk* is typically done by conventional banks. This is not because Islamic banks do not wish to take this role on, but because a market maker is always required to quote firm bid and offer prices, even when they do not hold any of the security, and is required to buy and or sell at the quoted prices. Due to the restrictions on selling an asset one does not own, an Islamic bank would not be able to provide a firm offer price for a *sukuk* issue the bank does not own, hence defeating the objective of providing liquidity in the market.

7.5 Syndication

Loan syndication services are offered to clients who require credit facilities which go beyond what can be provided by a single institution. There are a number of roles in the syndication process each with a different level of involvement. The bank taking on the majority of the work, and often the largest stake in the transaction is the lead arranger or book runner whose role encompasses the following:

- Negotiation and preparation of the term sheet, documents, and information memorandum;
- Interaction with potential interested parties throughout the syndications process;
- Resolution of issues related to closing and funding;
- Ongoing assistance with potential waiver and amendment requests that occur after the initial loan closing.

The main reason for banks to join a syndicate is risk mitigation, which is achieved by the fact that the banks in the syndicate share the risk of large, indivisible investment projects. Similar to conventional banks, Islamic banks participate in syndicated transactions, and do so for the same reasons which are summarised below:

- **Diversification of exposures.** By participating in syndications, a bank can diversify its investments and avoid excessive single-name exposure. In addition, it can be applied when a bank is looking to reduce some of its exposure in order to take on new business or to facilitate a strategic redirection.

- **Diversification of income.** Different types of fees such as agency and underwriting fees apply which do not only enhance the return on a transaction, they also result in a diversification of the fee income of the participants.

- **Relationship Management with clients and other banks.** The lead arranger maintains a close relationship with the client and has a strong view on other financial requirements. From the lead arranger's perspective it is important to maintain this relationship. For other members in the syndicate, it could be important to be affiliated with either the client or the lead arranger for future business, or from a reputational perspective. Additional financial opportunities may arise between the banks.

- **Flexibility.** Not only can any instrument outlined in chapter 4 be subject to syndication, the conditions are also highly negotiable. Underlying assets, collateral, documentation and repayment structures can all be adapted to the specific requirements of the transaction. In addition, the amount of financing that can be raised is flexible and not solely depending on the credit appetite of an individual institution.

- **Market entry.** Syndication provides an easy entry into a particular market for debut borrowers who can benefit from the knowledge and expertise of the lead arranger and other parties in the syndicate.

- **Comparative advantages.** Each of the members in the syndicate brings different advantages to the table in terms of financing. In addition, the book runner typically has much greater insight into market conditions and pricing affecting the client which other participants benefit from.

- **Reputation.** A well run syndication can raise a bank's profile significantly, resulting in further business opportunities.

The syndication process itself is in all respects similar to the conventional bank syndication process, with the sole exception that the underlying transactions have to be *sharia'a* compliant. In summary, the syndication process can generally be described along the following three phases[13]:

1. **Pre Mandate.** During this phase, the borrower approaches different institutions to provide an offer to arrange and manage the syndication. Based on the offers, taking into consideration the ability to attract participants, structuring capability and experience the borrower appoints one or more arrangers and mandates them to form the syndicate. The preliminary terms of the transaction are negotiated which include, but are not restricted to, amount, tenor, repayment structure and collateral.

2. **Post Mandate.** The arranger and the borrower prepare an information memorandum which contains an overview of the facility, sector, credit worthiness of the borrower and key transaction details. The information memorandum is shared with potentially interested market participants. Interested banks are requested to confirm the amount they would like to participate with by the deadline. Once the deadline is reached, the arranger allocates shares in the syndicated transaction to the individual banks.

3. **Post Completion.** The transaction is now active and becomes operational and is binding on both the syndicate and the borrower.

---

[13] Esty, B., 2001. Structuring loan syndicates: A case study of the Hong Kong Disneyland project loan. Journal of Applied Corporate Finance 14, 80–95

8 Application of Islamic Products in Corporate Finance

The definition of "corporate finance" varies considerably across the world[14], with the United States probably using the broadest definition. Generally, corporate finance describes activities, decisions and techniques that deal with many aspects of a company's finances and capital.

Corporate finance includes, but is not restricted to activities associated with: capital and debt-raising; the financing of joint ventures; project finance; infrastructure finance; public-private partnerships and privatisations; financing of management buy-outs; restructuring debt; and other forms of working capital financing.

The activities a bank undertakes as part of corporate finance depends on their internal structure and the country they are based in. The remainder of this chapter outlines some of the functions and provides examples of how Islamic financial products can be applied.

8.1 Trade Finance

The trade finance division typically arranges bespoke and structured financing arrangements to provide trade and inventory financing solutions. Inventory and stock finance, receivables finance, international trade finance and working capital finance are all part of the financial services offered by the trade finance division. Trade finance, which is generally associated with any form of trade, is, like the majority of activities within corporate finance, very well suited to the *sharia'a* principles due to the fact there is an asset flow underlying the transaction. Islamic banks issue guarantees and letters of credit, just like their conventional counterparts, although contrary to conventional finance a guarantee can not attract a charge. Besides letters of credit and guarantees, Islamic banks typically apply the following transaction types when it comes to trade finance:

- *Murabaha* **or deferred payment sales**. This transaction type is particularly suitable for inventory and stock finance in which the bank purchases the stock and sells it to the client on a deferred payment basis.

---

[14] The Institute of Chartered Accountants in England and Wales:
http://www.icaew.com/index.cfm/route/122299/icaew_ga/en/Technical_amp_Busine ss_Topics/Faculties/About_the_faculty/What_is_corporate_finance

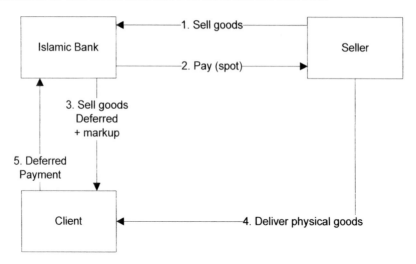

Figure 29: *Murabaha* in trade finance

Because the client has better knowledge of the market than the bank, the client, more often than not, acts as an agent negotiating the price and quality of the purchase. All details of the transaction are fully transparent to the client and the bank including the original purchase price, the mark up and the repayment date. Although the title to the goods transfers from the seller to the Islamic bank, the physical goods are generally delivered directly to the client on the instruction of the bank.

There can however be VAT implications attached to this structure, which vary on a country by country basis.

- ***Ijara* or lease.** Leasing transactions, as described in section 4.3.2.2, can be applied to finance plant or equipment. Finance lease, operating lease and sale and lease back structures can be offered, combined with fixed or floating rental payments. The lessee pays the rentals from the income the asset generates.

- ***Tawarruq***. From a regulatory and tax perspective, it is not always possible to apply any of the above mentioned structures in which case banks may have to resort to applying the *tawarruq* structure. As described in section 7.1.3, *tawarruq* is a variety of the commodity *murabaha*, in which a commodity – usually a base metal – is purchased and sold in order to generate a cash flow. Although there are notable issues with *tawarruq* transactions, the majority of *sharia'a* scholars approve of *tawarruq* as long as an auditable ownership transfer of the commodity and separation of the purchase and sale arrangements is taking place.

Graphically, the *tawarruq* can be depicted as follows:

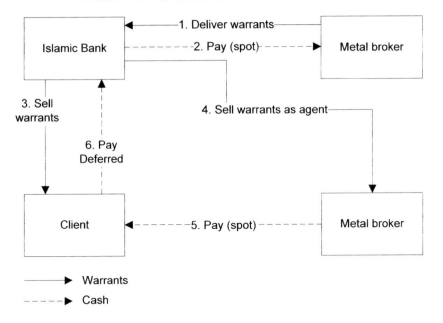

Figure 30: *Tawarruq* in trade finance

Although *tawarruq* may not be the most perfect instrument and has serious *sharia'a* issues associated with it, it does serve a purpose when Value Added Tax (VAT), stamp duty or other taxation rules pose limitations on Islamic finance and the *tawarruq* is more often than not the only feasible transaction type available.

8.2 Project Finance

The project finance division of a bank provides customers with financial advisory, arranging, structuring and underwriting services for limited-recourse project financing on a *sharia'a* compliant basis. Customers are wide ranging and include sponsors, contractors and public sector authorities. Project finance in Islamic finance will, like all other aspects of Islamic finance, have to comply with *sharia'a* principles. Although some projects are financed in a fully *sharia'a* compliant way, it is more common to see Islamic tranches within conventional project finance transactions, which is mainly to do with the fact that currently the transaction size is generally too large for Islamic financial institutions to handle.

Sectors requiring project finance include:

- Infrastructure and Public Private Partnerships (PPP)
- Transportation infrastructure and Shipping

- Water, Waste and Environmental
- Oil & Gas
- Petrochemicals
- Power and Energy, including Renewable Energy
- Telecommunications

The remainder of this section provides more detail on project finance and its development and the *sharia'a* compliant transaction types that can be applied.

8.2.1 What is Project Finance?[15]

In its basic form, project finance can be defined as:

> "A funding structure that relies on future cashflow from a specific development as the primary source of repayment with that development's assets rights and interests legally held as collateral security"[16]

A more accurate definition for a new project or development would be:

> "Project Financing is an option granted by the financier exercisable when an entity demonstrates that it can generate cashflows in accordance with long term cashflow forecasts. Upon exercise of the option, the entity's parent(s) or sponsor company(s) balance sheet is no longer available for debt service. The assets, rights and interests of the development are usually structured into a special purpose project vehicle (SPV) and are legally secured to the financiers as collateral"[17]

Historically major infrastructure projects were not undertaken by governments but by entrepreneurs using private investments. The development of railways is a good example. In 1891 Mr Jean Louis Pierson and his investment firm arranged the financing for a rail road in Manitoba which is in the southern part of Canada. Not only did he get paid a profit share on his investment, he also had a station named after him which over time developed into a town. Not only railways, but also roads, bridges, power plants, ports, water works and gas-distribution systems were being built all over the world by private entrepreneurs. These projects were financed largely by private capital, provided by entrepreneurs willing to risk all in return for high rewards. Some

---

15 This section provides an overview of project finance based on the information available from the International Project Finance Association (IPFA). For further detail see: http://www.ipfa.org/
16 Tinsley C.R. "Introduction and Glossary" Practical Introduction to Project Finance Euromoney Books, 1996
17 Tinsley C.R Advanced Project Financing, Structuring Risk First Edition, Euromoney Books, 2000

were profitable, but others were not. Projects that were privately financed included ambitious projects such as the Suez Canal and the Trans-Siberian Railway.

Over time, private sector entrepreneurship disappeared and projects were financed through public-sector borrowing with the state and public-utility organisations as the main clients. After World War II most infrastructure projects in industrialised countries were built under the supervision of the state and funded out of sovereign borrowings and tax revenues.

Project finance is seen an alternative source of funding for both small and large infrastructure and industrial projects. As a financing technique, it was perfected in the 1970s, and is now applied globally to a wide variety of privately promoted infrastructure projects including power stations, gas pipelines, waste-disposal plants, waste-to-energy plants, telecommunication facilities, bridges, tunnels, toll roads, railway networks, city-centre tram links, and the building of hospitals, education facilities, government accommodation and tourist facilities.

During the 1980s, governments started to review opportunities to privatise some of their activities and services, recognising the fact that private companies are motivated by profits which in turn leads to enhanced efficiency and productivity as well as the ability to implement projects more efficiently. This has in turn led to the development of what is commonly known as BOOT in which projects are financed on a limited-resource basis and built and then operated under a concession from the state or similar public body as a private venture. At the end of the concession the project is transferred back to the state or public body.

BOOT is a method to involve the private sector in large scale infrastructure investments and consists of the following components:

- **Build.** During this phase of the contract, the asset is built by the contractor who takes on the responsibility for constructing the asset and is expected to build the project on time, within budget and according to a clear specification.

- **Own.** During the lifetime of the concession, the concessionaire owns or possesses the assets. A concession agreement between the government and the concessionaire governs the extent to which ownership and control of the asset lies with the concessionaire. An ownership component is not always preferred. It is for instance not preferable for the concessionaire to own a hospital, hence giving him the right to change the use of the building if he feels other purposes could be more profitable.

- **Operate.** An operator will maintain the asset and operate it on a basis that maximises profits or minimises costs on behalf of the concessionaire during the lifetime of the concession.

- **Transfer.** At the end of the concession period, the asset reverts to the government. The transfer may be at book value or free of charge depending on the conditions of the concession.

There are a few varieties on this theme as listed below, some of which do not have an ownership component:

- BOO – Build, Own, Operate
- BOT – Build, Own, Transfer or Build, Operate, Transfer
- BRT – Build, Rent, Transfer
- BLT – Build, Lease, Transfer
- BT – Build, Transfer; and
- BTO- Build, Transfer, Operate

Over time, financial markets have become increasingly sophisticated in structuring financing packages to finance almost any type of reasonably predictable revenue stream.

In addition, Public Private Partnerships (PPP) and Private Finance Initiatives (PFI) have been developed where the emphasis is not on developing an asset, but more on providing a service although a capital expenditure component of some kind over the life of the concession is typically required.

PPP/PFI – An Example

The contract to maintain the A69 Carlisle – Newcastle, an 84 kilometre stretch of single and dual carriage way, was awarded to a consortium of six companies operating under the name Road Link for a period of 30 years.

Road Link's concession included the construction of the Haltwhistle Bypass and the operation and ongoing maintenance of the existing road. The payments are calculated on the number of vehicle kilometres travelled on the road, there is no direct payment of tolls by road users.

The Bypass (built to relieve traffic using the A69 through Haltwhistle and reduce accident, congestion, air pollution, noise and vibration) is approximately 3.5 kilometres long and required the construction of three major structures; two bridge crossings of the river South Tyne and a bridge crossing the Newcastle to Carlisle Railway[18].

8.2.2 Appropriate Islamic products

Project finance transactions are generally of a significant size and scale and are often financed by a consortium of multiple financial institutions. The most appropriate *sharia'a* compliant structure depends on the size of the project in combination with whether the whole project is financed in a *sharia'a* compliant way, or only a slice of the project is financed this way. When selecting the most appropriate structure, tax and legal issues will need to be taken into consideration. The following are the most commonly used structures:

- **Syndicated partnership transactions**

    Both the *mudaraba* or passive partnership and *musharaka* or active partnership as described in section 4.3 are suitable for project finance. When multiple banks are involved, the transaction could be offered on a syndicated basis. The financier typically does not get actively involved in the running of the partnership and is, in the case of a *musharaka*, usually a sleeping partner. From the financier's perspective, a *musharaka* structure will be preferable due to the fact that all partners provide a share of the capital.

    Musharaka transactions need to consist of at least two parties, and all partners are known as *musharik*.

---

18 This information is a summary of the full project information available on the Highways Agency's website: http://www.highways.gov.uk/roads/projects/5222.aspx, http://www.highways.gov.uk/roads/projects/5095.aspx

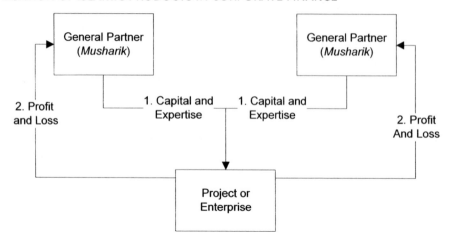

Figure 31: *Musharaka* transaction for project finance

Once the contract has been agreed between the partners, the process can be broken down into the following two main components:

1. **Cash and Expertise.** All partners provide a share of capital and expertise.

2. **Profits and Losses.** Profits are shared between the partners according to the ratios agreed in the contract. Any losses are distributed in proportion to capital contributions, although in the event of negligence all losses are borne by the managing party. The provider of funds will seek to limit his exposure by applying collateral and other risk mitigating convenants.

The underlying project is usually transferred to one of the participating partners, due to which a diminishing *musharaka* could be a suitable structure. As described in section 4.3.1.1, in a diminishing *musharaka* transaction the project is sold to one of the partners over the lifetime of the transaction.

- ***Istisna* for the build period combined with a lease**

In order to cover the build, own and operate phases, the project financing could be structured as a combination of a long term production finance (*istisna*) contract for the build phase in combination with a lease for the own and operate phases. This transaction can be structured as a syndicated facility, but could equally be wrapped up in a *sukuk*.

Graphically this transaction can be depicted as follows:

APPLICATION OF ISLAMIC PRODUCTS IN CORPORATE FINANCE

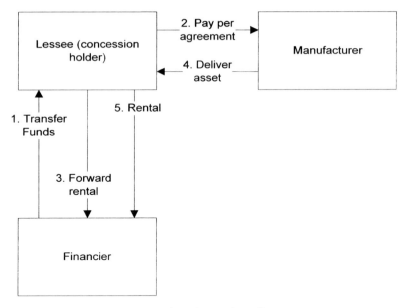

Figure 32: *Istisna* in project finance

The specification and cost of the asset are agreed between the concession holder and the contractor under an *istisna* contract. The funds are usually drawn by the concession holder as and when payments to the contractor are required. During the build period, the concession holder pays a forward rental fee to the financier. Once the asset is finished, the concession holder takes possession of the physical asset for the operate phase, and passes the title of the asset to the financier. During this phase, the concession holder leases the asset from the financier. At the end of the concession period, the asset is transferred to the ultimate owner, which is usually a government.

The risks to the financier are the same as the risks incurred in conventional project finance, and include but are not restricted to the following:

- Delays during the construction of the asset due to unforeseen circumstances, although this is typically mitigated by the date certain construction contracts with liquidated damages provisions;

- Cost overruns, although usually the construction contract is fixed price, not all components can always be fixed;

- Political risk consisting of adverse legislation or expropriation, currency inconvertibility and war or civil unrest. This risk can be mitigated by taking out insurance cover;

- FX risk, in the event more than one currency is involved;

ISLAMIC BANKING AND FINANCE   97

- Asset can not be delivered by the contractor;
- Lessee can not pay rentals;
- Asset becomes impaired;
- Operational risk when the performance of revenue realisation is below expectation.

8.2.3 The Project Finance Market

In the current market, projects outside the Middle East and Asia are generally not subject to Islamic finance structures, and even in those jurisdictions the Islamic finance component is, more often than not, only a slice of the total financing required. The size of the majority of project finance transactions is at the moment still prohibitive for Islamic financial institutions due to the fact that Islamic banks generally have a relatively small asset based in comparison with conventional banks.

Outside the Middle East and Asia, concession holders and banks are starting to consider including Islamic financial tranches into their project finance structures to enable them to access Middle Eastern capital and to diversify their sources of funding.

Currently, the majority of Islamic project finance has been in Middle East region, with a main focus on the GCC. In the current market, conventional banks are limited in their ability to finance, and borrowers and their advisers considering alternatives including Islamic finance. In addition, other markets such as North Africa are opening up more.

A combined *istisna* and *ijara* structure is most commonly applied, and as described above works well for project finance. Transactions with specific identifiable assets are easiest to structure e.g. a power station or process plant such as petrochemical plant, although there is no reason why assets such as roads should not be able to be financed this way.

A recent example of Islamic project finance is the Doraleh Container Terminal in Djibouti which is being financed through a *musharaka* with an underlying *istisna* and *ijara* structure

8.3 Property Finance

Property finance within corporate finance goes beyond the individual home purchase plans, and deals with the funding of large real estate purchases. Although property finance can include the purchase of stately homes and building new developments, it is certainly not limited to that and also encompasses commercial real estate such as shopping malls, gardening centres, hotels and office blocks. From an Islamic finance perspective real estate is a very suitable asset class and is favoured by many investors.

8.3.1 Property Finance – A Practitioners View

This section provides an overview of property finance in practice and is contributed by Allan Griffiths who joined BLME in 2007 after a long career in the conventional market. It represents his view on the Islamic financial market and is based on his own experiences.

Contributed by Allan Griffiths
Head of Property Finance BLME[19]

As a commercial property lender with a career in conventional banking spanning more than 20 years, my experience in joining an Islamic bank in the second half of 2007 has proven to be fascinating and has brought with it an extremely steep learning curve!

My first surprise was to discover just how much demand there is for Islamic property finance. Several recent events appear to have combined to create a significant increase in demand for Islamic financial products:

First, there is a strong political will in the UK to create a level playing field for Islamic finance. There appear to be three drivers for this:

- The need to make almost 2 million Muslims in the UK feel more included in UK society.

- A desire to ensure that the City of London maintains its dominance as a global financial centre.

- A growing government need to access funding from Middle Eastern entities, leading to a need to issue Sukuk.

The potential to issue the first UK Government *sukuk* is going through an elaborate consultation process to ensure all parties involved are aware of the potential challenges and benefits. Other practical measures so far taken by the Government to encourage Islamic finance are the abolition of double stamp duty land tax (SDLT) on Islamic mortgages and efforts to rectify the adverse effect of value added tax on Islamic financial products. The abolition of double SDLT has been a significant move for Islamic property finance solutions.

---

[19] Previously published in Business Islamica (April 2008) – *In Demand, Islamic Commercial Property Lending,* p. 43 – 44

However, additional regulation is (at the time of publishing this book) still required regarding VAT and capital gains tax (CGT) issues involved in the issue of debt and *sukuk* in the UK be it Government or Corporate.

Secondly, the US subprime debacle and the subsequent global aftermath have resulted in many conventional banks severely curtailing their lending activity in the property sector, which has caused many debt-driven investors to look for new sources of funding. One can't be involved in property finance without talking to the Jewish community, and interestingly, my existing non-Muslim clients have all been very supportive and willing to use Islamic finance. A typical comment was, "It's economic. If the product works and the price is right, there is no reason why we wouldn't deal with you."

And finally, there is a very strong Muslim investor community in the UK who have had to borrow conventionally in the past just because there was no other alternative available to them. However, with the establishment of Islamic banks in the UK, and the availability of Islamic finance via windows of conventional banks, these investors are now provided with a choice. As a consequence, we are seeing many new opportunities from this source, not only for property finance but for a wide range of financial structures.

Development / Mezzanine Finance
In my past life as a conventional banker working for the London branches of overseas banks (which were mainly German), I was mostly involved in big-ticket senior debt transactions funding standing investment property and was hardly ever involved in equity or mezzanine arrangements or development finance.

As a consequence of Islamic ideas about risk sharing and because of the fact that Islamic banks currently have relatively small balance sheets compared to conventional banks, Islamic banks are much more interested in equity and mezzanine finance opportunities. From a personal point of view, I find this type of finance much more rewarding because it enables me to take a holistic approach and work in partnership with our customers. To state the obvious, every deal needs 100 percent funding from somewhere, but typically, there is a gap between the equity contribution our client can make out of his own funds and the level of senior debt available to him. Our job is to bridge that gap. It's no coincidence that the Bank of London and The Middle East logo is a stylised bridge. I think this approach is much appreciated by our customers, who generally say that they find it a refreshing change from the conventional approach, and it does give rise to some very interesting opportunities and challenges. For example, we have recently completed a transaction in which the senior debt is provided conventionally, with an Islamic mezzanine tranche being provided by BLME.

It's also worth noting that a considerable amount of research and product development is taking place right now, so the range of available *sharia'a*-compliant products and techniques is expanding all the time.

Property Funds

Another area of business which has huge potential for Islamic banks is the management of property funds to be set up and managed on behalf of clients. For example, in one case I am currently involved with, a public sector institution wants to invest in UK property. The company has a requirement for a regular steady income stream from the fund, but also wants an overall return of 8 percent per annum. In order to achieve this, we are planning to assemble a portfolio of core income-producing institutional-quality assets. The remainder of the fund will be used to fund equity positions in commercial developments in prime town centre locations. This part of the fund will be geared to enhancing returns further. With oil between $100 and $120 per barrel in September 2008, the demand from Middle East entities for fund management and investment services in London looks set to increase substantially over the next few years.

Market View

Until recently, the UK commercial property market had seen an unprecedented period of sustained growth over the past decade or so. This had been underpinned, at least in part, by a low-inflation environment which was achieved in 1997 by transferring responsibility for setting interest rates from the Chancellor of the Exchequer to the Monetary Policy Committee of the Bank of England and, at the same time, setting the Monetary Policy Committee a monthly inflation target.

However, the subprime crisis proved to be the shock which triggered a loss of confidence in UK commercial property values and a sharp reversal in yield trends resulted. This in turn caused many journalists to liberally use emotive words such as "crash" and "slump." Whilst a downturn is always steeper than the upslope and therefore seemingly more alarming, it is nevertheless an integral feature of a cyclical market. We should never forget that the property market is inherently cyclical. If you believe that the upslope is a straight line which carries on forever, you will invariably lose money.

There is currently a lively debate amongst some of the market commentators as to whether the market has bottomed out or whether there is more bad news to follow. Nevertheless, it is the case that property in the UK at the moment looks cheap in comparison with other major European destinations and offers a substantial number of investment opportunities.

In the City of London, development activity continues at a high level, with some streets looking like large building sites, and it remains to be seen how robust tenant demand proves to be. My guess is that is that it will remain quite strong, because if it starts to weaken, some intended developments will just be mothballed until the next cycle.

8.3.2 Suitable Transaction Types

Not all transaction types explored in chapter 4 are suitable for large scale property finance. This section explores the potential ways of funding real estate and reviews the reason why the most used transaction type is the one scholars like the least, the *tawarruq*.

For real estate already in existence, there are three main transaction types suitable to provide funding.

- *Murabaha* **or deferred payment sale.** Similar to the *murabaha* transaction described in section 4.3.2.1, the bank purchases the property and sells it on to the client for a deferred payment which consists of the principal plus a mark up. The mark up can be paid to the bank on a periodic basis. The main drawback of this transaction type is its lack of flexibility in payment structures and extension possibilities. The mark up is fixed for the duration of the contract and the contract can not be extended. If the client requires an extension of the funding, the first contract will have to be paid back after which the bank and the client can enter into a new contract.

- *Ijara* **or lease.** In this contract, the bank will purchase the property and acts as the lessor to lease the property to the client, most likely under a finance lease construction as described in section 4.3.2.2 and shown below:

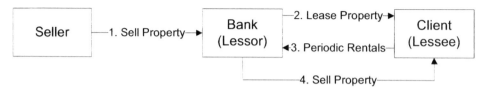

Figure 33: Lease applied to property finance

Alternatively, a sale and lease back could be considered in which the client purchases the property, sells it to the bank and leases it back, as shown below:

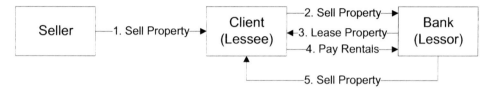

Figure 34: Sale and lease back applied to property finance

In both cases, the rental payments could include an amount towards the purchase price of the property, and rentals can either be fixed or reviewed periodically.

- **Diminishing *musharaka* or reducing partnership.** In this scenario, the bank and the client both invest in the property, and the property is divided in equal units which the client will purchase from the bank over time. Similar to the diminishing *musharaka* detailed in section 4.3.1.1, the purchase of units by the client is flexible and can be arranged in the contract. The client pays a rental fee for the part of the property he does not own which can be reviewed periodically.

Each of the above transaction types can be applied, although the lease and the diminishing *musharaka* offer significantly more flexibility for both the bank and the clients.

For new developments, the above transaction types are not suitable since the property is neither owned, nor in existence. As a result, new developments require a different approach to meet the funding requirements. The financing of new developments can for instance be funded as follows:

- ***Salam* or short term production finance.** As described in section 4.3.2.3, the *salam* contract is a purchase contract for future delivery of an asset and is exempt from the conditions regarding ownership and existence of the asset. At the time of contracting, the asset does not yet have to exist, and it does not have to be owned by the seller. When applying a *salam* contract to property finance, the bank provides the full amount of funding up front and will be paid out of the proceeds of the sale of the property.

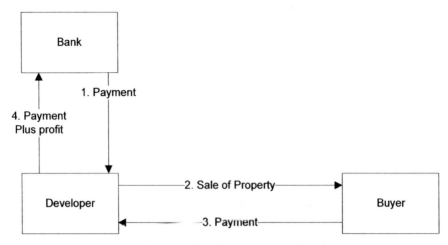

Figure 35: *Salam* for property development

The developer repays the bank out of the proceeds of the sale on a pre-agreed date in the future. The disadvantage of a *salam* transaction applied to property development is that there is no flexibility in the contract itself. The full amount has to be paid upfront and delivery of the asset has to take place on a pre-agreed date. Due to the fact that financial regulators typically do not look favourably on banks taking any exposure to commodities, the transaction will be structured as such that the developer takes responsibility for the sale of the property to an end buyer and the payment from the developer to the bank will be the principal plus profit.

* ***Istisna* or long term production finance.** Like a *salam* contract, an *istisna* contract is a purchase contract for future delivery of an asset, and is exempt from the same two conditions regarding the asset, ownership and existence. In an *istisna* contract, the payment to the property developer does not have to be in full in advance. Payment is likely to be in various instalments in line with the progress made. The *istisna* contract is typically for a longer term than a *salam* contract.

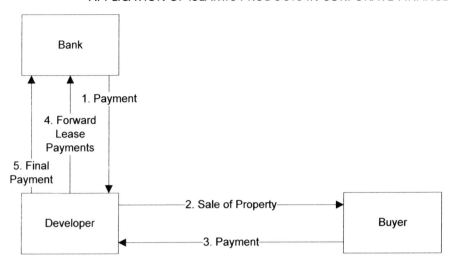

Figure 36: *Istisna* in property finance, financing developer

Under the *istisna* structure depicted in the figure above, it is assumed that there is a third party ultimate buyer who has sufficient funds available to pay for the asset as and when payment is required. The buyer could for instance obtain these funds by entering into a mortgage contract. Given that the bank is unlikely to be willing to wait until the development is sold, it is often agreed in the contract that the property developer pays forward lease payments during the construction period. These payments are made out of the sales proceeds. A final payment from the developer to the bank at the end of the period could be part of the structure.

In the transaction outlined above, it is assumed that the property will be sold on to an ultimate buyer and that financing is only required during the construction period. Alternatively, the buyer could be the bank's client, in which case the transaction can be depicted as follows:

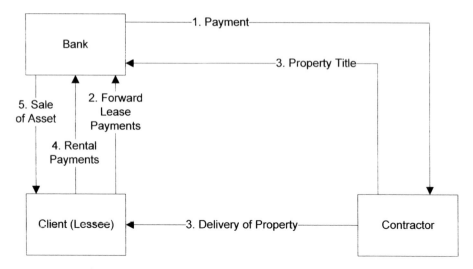

Figure 37: *Istisna* in property finance, financing end client

In this structure, the following steps take place:

1. **Payment**. From the bank to the contractor or developer, in accordance with the contract.

2. **Forward Lease**. The end buyer pays forward lease payments during the construction phase of the property.

3. **Delivery of property**. The property title is delivered to the bank who becomes the lessor, and the client, who becomes the lessee, takes delivery of the property itself. Once the property is delivered, the forward lease ceases to exist and the lease comes in effect.

4. **Rental payments**. The client pays periodic rentals to the bank for the duration of the lease. The rentals may include a payment towards ownership of the asset.

5. **Sale of asset**. At the end of the lease, the client buys the asset from the bank.

Compared to the *salam* contract, the *istisna* contract is more flexible due to the fact that payment terms can be negotiated to meet the requirements of the client and the property developer. In addition, by introducing staged payments in line with progress, there is an additional incentive for the developer to manage the building process efficiently.

Although the above mentioned transaction types are preferable from an Islamic finance and *sharia'a* perspective, they can not automatically be applied in every jurisdiction. Issues with double stamp duty land tax and VAT can make these types of funding very tax inefficient and hence less attractive to the client. In order to enable the funding of property therefore, the *tawarruq* structure is often favoured by banks and clients alike. As described in section 7.1.3, *tawarruq* is a variety of the commodity *murabaha*, in which a commodity – usually a base metal – is purchased and sold in order to generate a cash flow. There are however, *sharia'a* issues with *tawarruq*. The main issue is the fact that the intention behind the purchase of the commodity is not to own and use the commodity, but solely to generate a cash flow. The majority of *sharia'a* scholars approve of *tawarruq* as long as an auditable ownership transfer of the commodity and separation of the purchase and sale arrangements is taking place.

Graphically, the *tawarruq* can be depicted as follows:

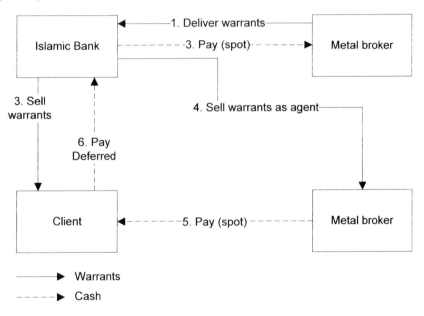

Figure 38: *Tawarruq* in property finance

In a *tawarruq* there is one agreement in which both parties agree that the Islamic bank will sell the warrants to the client and simultaneously sell them to a metal broker on behalf of the client. Due to the fact that sale, purchase and appointing the bank as agent are all happening in one schedule, it is almost impossible to see who owns the commodity at any point during the execution of the transaction. Consequently, if the transaction falls through at any point, ownership of the asset is not clear. The majority of *sharia'a* scholars approve of *tawarruq* as long as an auditable ownership transfer of the commodity and separation of the purchase and sale arrangements is taking place.

Although *tawarruq* may not be the most perfect instrument and has serious *sharia'a* issues associated with it, it does serve a purpose when Value Added Tax (VAT), stamp duty or other taxation rules pose limitations on Islamic finance and the *tawarruq* is more often than not the only feasible transaction type available.

8.4 Leasing

By their nature, leasing transactions always have an underlying asset and are based on risk and reward sharing, which makes them extremely suitable for Islamic finance. As described in section 4.3.2.2, an *ijara* transaction is the Islamic equivalent of a lease, which is defined as a bilateral contract allowing for the transfer of the usufruct. This means that one party (the lessor) allows another party (the lessee) to use his asset against the payment of a rental fee. Within Islamic finance, two types of leasing transactions exist, operating and finance leases. *Ijara* is the general term for lease and signifies an operational lease. *Ijara wa iqtina* is a lease ending in ownership and is equivalent to a finance lease. Within Islamic finance the assets that are subject to a lease are varied, and include car fleets, trucks, ships and machinery.

Although Islamic leasing transactions are typically based on *sharia'a* compliant legal documentation, there are situations where this is legally not possible for instance due to the jurisdiction of the client. In the event conventional leasing documentation needs to be applied, the Islamic bank and the client can opt to have an additional contract in place that deals with anything that is not *sharia'a* compliant such as penalty clauses and insurance. For example, it is not permissible to charge a late paying client a penalty over and above the cost incurred by the bank to address this issue. If a penalty interest clause is included in the contract, the bank can collect these but will have to give them to charity. The responsibility for insuring the asset is typically passed on to the lessee via an agency agreement.

A typical leasing structure can be represented as follows:

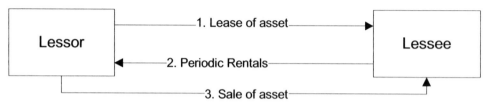

Figure 39: Finance lease

An operating lease is similar, but does not have a sale of the asset to the lessee incorporated in the structure.

8.4.1 Determination of Rental Payments

The rental amount due on a lease incorporates a variety of different factors which are summarised below.

Component	Finance Lease	Operating Lease
Term, repayment profile and payment in advance or in arrears	√	√
Deduction or inclusion of servicing fees	√	√
Fees and commissions payable	√	√
Cost of Funds	√	√
Counterparty credit risk	√	√
Value of the underlying asset	√	√
Country and other risks	√	√
Residual Value Risk		√
Residual Value Realisation		√

Table 3: Rental payment components

The residual value is only of importance in an operating lease since the lessor takes a view on the value at which he can sell the asset at the end of the lease term.

In an operating lease, the lessee and lessor have the following options at the end of the lease term:

1. **Renew the lease.** In this case, the lease is extended for the same rental amount on the same equipment. The lessee typically only does this if it is more beneficial to his operation than returning the asset and leasing a new one.

2. **Return asset to lessor.** If the lessee no longer wishes to use the asset it can be returned to the lessor at the end of the lease period. The lessor can then chose to lease the same asset to a different counterparty, or sell it in the market.

3. **Purchase at fair market value.** The lessee can request to buy the asset from the lessor at the current market value.

9 The Application of Islamic Products to Private Equity

Private Equity is not always a separate division within a bank, but can also occur as part of the corporate finance division or treasury. Due to the fact that private equity investments represent a direct investment in an enterprise and the investor is taking a business risk, investments in public as well as private equity are looked upon favourably by *sharia'a* scholars. The two different structures as described in chapter 4 that are suitable for private equity investments are *musharaka* and *mudaraba* type transactions.

In a joint venture of *musharaka* structure, all partners provide capital and skill and expertise to the project. Profits are shared based on a contractually agreed ratio between the partners and any losses are distributed in accordance with the proportion of capital provided. The bank often opts to become a sleeping partner and leaves running of the business to the other partners, potentially in return for a lower share in the profits.

Musharaka transactions are typically suitable for investments in business ventures or specific business projects, and need to consist of at least two parties, and all partners are known as *musharik*.

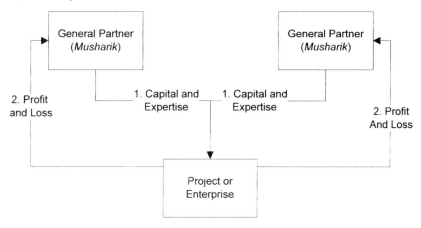

Figure 40: *Musharaka* transaction for Private Equity

Another option for private equity investment besides the *musharaka* transaction, is the *mudaraba,* a partnership in which only one of the partners contributes capital (the *rab al mal*), and the other (the *mudarib*) contributes skill and expertise. Like the *musharaka* transaction, the profits are shared between the partners according to the ratios agreed in the original contract. Any losses are solely attributable to the investor due to the fact that he is the sole provider of all capital to the project. In the event of a loss, the business manager does not receive any compensation (*mudarib* share) for his efforts. The only exception to this is when the business manager has been negligent, in which case he becomes liable for the total loss.

Contrary to the *musharaka* in which partners have unlimited liability, the investor or *rab al mal* in a *mudaraba* transaction is only liable to the extent of the capital he has provided. As a result, the business manager or *mudarib* can not commit the business for any sum which is over and above the capital provided.

10 The Role of the London Metal Exchange

The underlying asset for commodity *murabaha* and *tawarruq* transactions is more often than not a base metal such as aluminium or nickel. The base metals are generally associated with the London Metal Exchange (LME) which is due to the fact that the exchange is by far the largest player in the market. Although not a physical market, the LME controls the issuance of warrants that represents ownership of the metal. The commodities in a commodity *murabaha* and *tawarruq* transaction are often referred to as "LME Base Metal" even though in their current form the contracts that are traded on the exchange is not an appropriate underlying asset to a transaction as will become clear from the remainder of this chapter.

10.1.1 The London Metal Exchange

Although trading of metals has taken place at the Royal Exchange since its opening in 1571, the London Metal Exchange Company was not established until 1877. The industrial revolution in the 18th and 19th century led to a significant increase in the demand for metal and a requirement for imports. The merchant sourcing these materials invested large sums of money and was exposed to high financial risk due to the fact that journeys were long and dangerous. In order to mitigate any risk of prices falling during the journey, a market developed in which metal could be sold for delivery at a future date estimated based on the ship's arrival time, at a price agreed on the trade date. The LME was established to formalise this process through the creation of a single market place with recognised trading times and standardised contracts.[20]

The LME is however not the natural source for physical metal. It is rather a financial futures market used mainly for limiting future price risk, supported by a delivery as a last resort. The warrants underlying the commodity *murabaha* transactions are not traded on the exchange, but are traded over the counter.

10.1.2 Warrants

The underlying asset to a commodity *murabaha* is typically any of the London Metal Exchange (LME) base metals ownership of which is represented by an LME warrant. An LME warrant is a certificate for a specific metric tonnage of an approved brand of metal stored in an LME approved warehouse. The

---

[20] For more information: www.lme.com

warrant is a bearer document and signifies ownership of the underlying metal to the holder. An LME warrant contains the following information:

- **LME Warrant identification.** This is the unique warrant number, warrant id and the date the warrant is created.

- **Location of warehouse.** Specifying the name and exact location of the warehouse, as well as the company operating the warehouse.

- **Metal details**. This includes the type of metal, the shape, brand, quantity, country of origin and net weight in kilos.

- **Rental and insurance**. The bearer of the warrant is due to pay an annual rent for storage of the metal which is included in the purchase price. In addition, the bearer has the responsibility to insure the metal.

An LME warrant is issued by a London agent on behalf of an LME approved warehouse upon receipt of the goods from the supplier. The physical warrants are stored in a specialised repository and do not leave the repository until they are checked out by the owner for physical delivery. Ownership of the warrants is registered in the SWORD system, a secure electronic transfer system which is developed as a joint initiative between the LME and the London Clearing House. All LME warrants are produced to a standard format with a barcode. Warehouse companies issuing these warrants ensure that the details are known to SWORD which acts as a central database, holding details of ownership and is subject to stringent security controls. The ownership of LME warrants can be transferred between SWORD members in a matter of seconds and all rent payments are automatically calculated.

Warrants are sold over the counter (OTC) and are available for a multitude of LME products, though not all are acceptable from a *sharia'a* perspective, since the underlying asset needs to be non-perishable. Plastic, for example, does not meet this requirement. Base metals, however, are widely accepted by *sharia'a* boards as an asset in a commodity *murabaha* as it is documented as a warrant in a warehouse.

From a commodity *murabaha* perspective, the warrants most often used are Aluminium and Copper. This is primarily because of the large contract size and relatively higher price per warrant which ensures the number of warrants to be purchased is low.

In commodity *murabaha* and *tawarruq* transactions, commodity price risk is avoided in two ways:

1. **Timing of purchase and sale.** All purchase and sale transaction of commodities take place on the same day.

2. **Premium warrants.** To mitigate the risk of any price movement during the day, the warrants that are used within these transactions are those that are trading at a premium to the market price. The reason that these warrants trade at a premium is often due to the location of the warehouse.

Warrant premiums – an example

In the course of a contract, a bridge builder in the north east of England has a requirement for 15,625 metric tonnes of Aluminium. A single warrant of Aluminium represents 25 metric tonnes, and as a result, he requires 625 warrants. The bridge builder will need the Aluminium to be delivered to the building side and has the following options:

- Buy 625 warrants at the current market price of USD 2,751 located in a warehouse in Singapore
- Buy 625 warrants at the premium price of USD 2,950 located in a warehouse in Tyne and Wear

Given the time involved in shipping the physical metal from Singapore and the associated cost, the bridge builder is likely to buy the premium price for the warrants which are stored near him.

10.2 LME Base Metals

Warrants are available for the following base metals:

Metal	Symbol	Description	Contract size*
Aluminium		Aluminium is light, nontoxic, and can be easily formed, machined and cast. Although in its purest form it is soft and lacks strength, but alloys with small amounts of copper, magnesium, silicon, manganese, and other elements have very useful properties.	25 Metric Tonnes
		Aluminium Alloy and NASAAC (North American Special Aluminium Alloy) are derivatives of Aluminium and trade in contract sizes of 20 Metric Tonnes	20 Metric Tonnes
Copper		Copper is reddish with a bright metallic lustre. It is malleable, ductile, and a good conductor of heat and electricity (second only to silver). The most important compounds are the oxide and the sulphate, (blue vitriol). It is relatively soft and moderately reactive	25 Metric Tonnes

Metal	Symbol	Description	Contract size*
Lead		Lead is a dense, relatively soft, malleable metal with low tensile strength. It is a poor conductor of electricity and heat	25 Metric Tonnes
Nickel		Nickel is a hard, malleable, ductile, lustrous, silver-white metal which exhibits magnetic properties and is a fairly good conductor of heat and electricity. The major use of Nickel is in its alloys.	6 Metric Tonnes
Zinc		Zinc is brittle and crystalline at ordinary temperatures, but when heated to between 110°C and 150°C it becomes ductile and malleable; it can then be rolled into sheets. It is used principally for galvanizing steel consumer goods	25 Metric Tonnes
Tin		Tin is very soft (only slightly harder than lead) and malleable; it can be rolled, pressed, or hammered into extremely thin sheets (tin foil). Its main commercial uses are in tinplating steel products for the food packaging industry.	5 Metric Tonnes
Plastic		Plastic is the general term for a wide range of synthetic or semi synthetic polymerisation products. There are many natural polymers generally considered to be "plastics" which can be formed into many different types of objects, films or fibers. The name is derived from the malleability, or plasticity, of many of them. The word derives from the Greek *plastikos*, of fit for molding, which in turn is derived from *plastos* which means molded.	24.75 Metric Tonnes
Steel		Steel is an alloy consisting mostly of iron, with carbon content between 0.2 and 2.04% by weight, depending on grade. Carbon is the most cost-effective alloying material for iron, but various other alloying elements are used.	65 Metric Tonnes

* Actual weight per warrant is in a range of plus or minus 2%

Table 4: LME Base Metals

11 Asset Management

Within Islam, investing in enterprises and assets is encouraged not because of the wealth increase for the individual investor, but also because it advances the economy and at the same time allows others to increase their wealth. This in turn results in better wealth distribution.

Conventional and Islamic investors have common objectives such as capital preservation, yield maximisation and ensuring a balance between liquidity and profitability in addition to which Islamic investors also look for *sharia'a* compliance. Not every investor has the time to manage their investments actively, and like conventional investors, Islamic investors often turn to fund or asset management solutions.

Like conventional investment managers, Islamic investment managers can invest in a wide range of Islamic and conventional products and asset classes including shares and other securities. The main difference between conventional and Islamic investment managers is that the latter will have to ensure that his individual investments, as well as his fund, remain compliant with *sharia'a*. In addition, Islamic fund managers can not use derivatives, pay or receive interest or apply stock lending techniques.

Fund structures are typically similar to conventional structures although again, *sharia'a* compliance is a key factor. A *Sharia'a* Supervisory Board, which is typically made up of three to five members, is involved from the start of the fund. The *Sharia'a* Supervisory Board is not responsible for any operational and strategic decisions the fund manager makes as long as the fund continues to be *sharia'a* compliant. The *Sharia'a* Supervisory Board is, however, involved in the definition of the framework the fund operates in and defines issues such as which industries are deemed compliant.

The remainder of this chapter outlines the AAOIFI *sharia'a* standards for the selection of *sharia'a* compliant investments and presents a view on how Islamic asset management can successfully be applied in practice.

11.1 Selection of Sharia'a compliant investments

When investing in a company, there are two basic screening processes that need to be applied prior to deciding whether or not a stock should be allowed to be part of the investment universe. Within *sharia'a*, a number of business activities are deemed to be *haram*, in which one should not invest.[21]

---

[21] AAOIFI *sharia'a* standard 21

11.1.1 Industry Screen

The first selection when deciding whether to accept a share in the investment universe is often referred to as the 'industry screen'. Although it is preferable to allow only fully *sharia'a* compliant funds in the universe, increasing globalisation, diversification and market demand does not always make this possible. As a result, a particular share or business can be a *sharia'a* compliant investment opportunity, even when an insignificant amount of their turn over is deemed to be *haram*. Although the definition of "insignificant" varies between *Sharia'a* Supervisory Boards, it is generally accepted to be five percent or less of total turnover.

The industry screen is meant to eliminate any *haram* businesses from the investment universe and excludes the following business activities:

- **Conventional Banking and Insurance.** Conventional banking and insurance is associated with interest and is therefore not permissible.
- **Alcohol.** The prohibition of alcohol extends to distilling, marketing and sale and includes working in the industry. Medicinal alcohol and alcohol used in the production of perfumes is not prohibited.
- **Pork related products and non-compliant food production.** Non-compliant food production covers everything which is not prepared in a *halal* way and covers, among others, meat which is not slaughtered in an acceptable fashion.
- **Gambling.** This covers casinos and betting shops, but also bingo halls and on-line betting.
- **Tobacco.** As with alcohol, this includes the production, marketing and sales of tobacco and associated products.
- **Adult entertainment.** Any activity associated with adult entertainment including escort services, brothels and movies with explicit sexual content.
- **Weapons, arms and defence manufacturing.**

These industries or sectors should not form part of the portfolio of any Islamic investor.

11.1.2 Financial Screen

In addition to the industry screen, companies that use too much leverage are also excluded from the investment universe. Although the exact financial ratios can vary by *Sharia'a* Supervisory Board, the generally accepted financial ratios are as follows[22]:

---

[22] AAOIFI *Sharia'a* Standard number 21

- Conventional Debt / Total Assets < 30%
- (Cash + Interest bearing deposits) / Total Assets < 30%
- Accounts receivables / Total Assets <= 45%
- (Total interest + income from non compliant activities) / Revenue < 5%

11.1.3 Application of the Industry and Financial Screen

Although not all scholars agree on this, the general approach is that any income from *haram* activities should be purified via the dividend payments. This is a pragmatic approach to allow Islamic funds to be set up and operate within the *sharia'a* framework. The *sharia'a* compliant indices that have been developed over time may use more lenient or more stringent criteria. Dow Jones for instance uses the following for the Dow Jones Islamic Markets Index (DJIM):

- **Industry Screen.** Exclude alcohol, tobacco, pork and pork related products, financial services, defence/weapons and entertainment.

- **Financial Screen.** The financial screens are all taken over market capitalisation and apply a 12 month rolling average to enable a smoother picture, and any firm should meet the following criteria:

  - Total debt / trailing 12 month average market capitalisation < 33%
  - (Cash + interest bearing securities) / trailing 12-month average market capitalisation < 33%
  - Accounts receivable / 12 month average market capitalisation < 33%

On the other hand, the FTSE Global Islamic Index Series (GIIS) applies the following rules:

- **Industry Screen.** Exclude alcohol, tobacco, pork and pork related products, banking or any other interest related activity, arms manufacturing, life insurance and gaming.

- **Financial Screen.** Any company within the index will have to pass the following criterion:

  - Gross Interest Bearing debt / total assets < 33%

  In addition, the FTSE GIIS specifically mentions that the percentage used represents the maximum allowed under *sharia'a* which is currently set at 33%.

The exact screening criteria applied to an individual fund or index strongly depend on the framework of the fund or index and the opinion of the *sharia'a* scholars.

ISLAMIC BANKING AND FINANCE   119

11.1.4 Non-Compliance

No matter how thorough the screening, a situation could occur where a share becomes (temporarily) non-compliant. It is the responsibility of the fund manager to report this to the *Sharia'a* Supervisory Board together with his recommendation on how to proceed. If the stock is deemed to be temporarily non-compliant, the *Sharia'a* Supervisory Board could allow the stock to remain part of the investment universe. All income from the stock in that period will need to be purified for as long as the non-compliance occurs.

Some *Sharia'a* Supervisory Boards however do not allow any period of non-compliance and a share that becomes non-compliant will need to be sold within a given number of days, whether it is expected to get back to become compliant or not. However, once a share is compliant again it can be added to the fund, although the fund manager will probably incorporate the fact that a share was non-compliant and the likelihood of this occurring again in his decision making.

Where permanent non-compliance occurs, divestment will always be required. However, within the framework of the fund, and in order to protect investor's interests, the *Sharia'a* Board is likely to allow this to be a phased process.

11.2 Types of Funds

The number of *sharia'a* compliant funds is increasing rapidly with new funds being announced on a regular basis. By far the majority of the currently available funds are structured as unit trusts or mutual funds, and in excess of 50% of funds invest in equity. Although most equity funds use some form of benchmark to track their performance against, the majority of funds appear to have an active management strategy. Unsurprisingly, the main investment geographies across different funds are Asia Pacific and The Middle East and Africa regions.

The average fund size at the moment is around $100 million which, compared to conventional funds is low. Only very few funds have assets under management of $500 million or over and can be considered benchmark size, and the majority of funds is currently operating in the $1 - $200 million size bracket.

11.3 Asset Management – A Practitioners View

This section provides an overview of asset management in practice and is contributed by Charles Peal who works with BLME in the fund management division. It represents his view on the Islamic funds market and is based on his own experiences.

A New Investment Style for Islamic Investors
Contributed by Charles Peal

Are you finding it easy to invest in size in financially attractive Islamic products, compliant with *sharia'a*? Are you aware of respected *sharia'a* indices that have produced benchmark returns of between 15% and 30% per annum for the last five years[23]? Has your fund's (net) performance beaten the lower end of this range?

If your answers to some or all of these questions is no, this section of the book is for you. We discuss some of the main issues you are facing, and share some of our investment management insights with you.

First, let's backtrack a little. At present a significant amount of the financial assets owned by Islamic investors are conventional, reflecting the lack of Islamic alternatives. The imbalance between the supply of and demand for *sharia'a* compliant product is a growing issue for Islamic investors.

Such imbalance was illustrated by a report published by the McKinsey Global Institute in October 2007. McKinsey estimated that the total value of global financial assets at the end of 2006 was $167 trillion, of which around $3.6 trillion were held by a number of countries described as "oil-rich".

Among the oil–rich, the smaller number of Gulf Cooperation Council states (Bahrain, Kuwait, Oman, Qatar, Saudi Arabia and the United Arab Emirates or the "UAE", collectively referred to below as the GCC) accounted for around half of the above total, with foreign assets of $1.6 - $2 trillion at the end of 2006.

Based on oil prices per barrel, McKinsey made the following estimates of how the foreign assets of oil-rich countries are expected to grow by 2012:

Price per Barrel	Projected foreign assets
$50	$5.9 trillion
$70	$7.9 trillion

Table 5: Oil price and projected foreign assets

---

[23] FTSE Group, as at 30 June 2008. FTSE Shariah indices are based on back tests

This implies that at an oil price of $70 per barrel, significant amounts flow into the countries of the Gulf Co-Operative Countries (GCC). In September 2008, the price of crude oil was around $100 – $120 per barrel, having come down from around $140 per barrel.

Some of these excess funds will need to be invested, and one of the options is to offer a combination of competitively priced passive equity index funds and active money market funds that satisfy investor demand, without sacrificing returns, while carefully following the *sharia'a* compliance process set out in the earlier paragraphs of this chapter. This combination could potentially result in two compelling reasons to switch to *sharia'a* compliant products; comparable performance at low cost.

11.3.1 Core and Satellite Asset Allocations

It makes good sense for Islamic and conventional investors to use the same type of asset allocation model to decide between core investments and satellite activities within their funds or portfolios.

Asset allocation models use the liabilities of a fund to determine the balance between the two core investment allocations, in other words the choice between holding cash and taking an equity-style risk. A fund with immediate liabilities tends to hold more in cash, so that its obligations can be met without undue short term volatility and risk. A fund with more distant liabilities on the other hand, tends to hold more in equities as, over time, equities have outperformed cash and conventional bonds[24].

In turn, the equity allocation of a fund can have two components, core allocations and satellite activities. Core funds aim to match the performance of a benchmark index, whereas satellite funds have the freedom to use more risky, benchmark-beating strategies in order to achieve a higher net return. Examples of satellite funds include actively managed listed equities, property funds and alternative assets, supplemented by any direct investments chosen by the investor without reference to an external fund manager. Both core and satellite funds should be measured against carefully chosen benchmarks, usually an index for a given geographic area or a particular stock market. Unfortunately, historic studies have shown it is generally beyond the ability of most (but not all) satellite fund managers to beat their benchmarks consistently, whether they are employing enhanced stock picking strategies, or using alternative asset strategies.

---

[24] Any investor will have to bear in mind that historic performance is no guarantee for future returns.

If investors were to place core equity allocations in *sharia'a* compliant index funds, the key investment decision becomes the choice of an index (or range of indices) that best suits the investment aims of the individual investor or that particular fund or portfolio.

Once core allocations to index funds are in place, a smaller proportion of equity risk can be allocated to satellite funds on a multi-manager basis. This process provides more flexibility to work on time-consuming but potentially highly rewarding satellite investments and provides the investor with a fair benchmark to calculate how much added value the satellite investments produce over the short to medium term.

A simple core and satellite asset allocation model for the Islamic portion of a fund with limited short term liabilities is set out below. Taken as a whole, this portfolio is designed to be 100% *sharia'a* compliant.

Example of a Simple Islamic Asset Allocation Model

	Proportion Core/Index	Proportion Satellite*	Total
Cash			
US Dollar	10%		10%
Other currencies	10%		10%
Equity Risk			
All World	40%	0%	40%
Developed Markets	10%	10%	20%
Emerging Markets	10%	10%	20%
TOTAL			**100%**

* Includes property funds, alternative assets and direct investments.

Table 6: Islamic Asset Allocation Model – Example

11.3.2 Secret 1: Index Trackers Consistently Outperform Active Funds

Here's our first vital secret: over the three years to 30 June 2008, the FTSE Shariah All World $ Index made a compound return of 14.75% per annum.

Few conventional asset management groups explain the compelling case for index funds. This is because most have a vested interest in promoting active fund management which earn higher fees and support high salaries and marketing expenditure. Although many expert investors have explained why index funds consistently outperform active funds, we believe their lessons are often forgotten or buried under new marketing material.

ASSET MANAGEMENT

The first index fund available to the general public, benchmarked to the S&P 500, was the Vanguard Investment Fund (since renamed the Vanguard 500 Index Fund) which was founded in 1976 by John C Bogle. Today this is one of the top performing US large cap funds and has attracted more than $100 billion of capital. It is worth recalling the benefits first identified by Vanguard and showing how apparently small differences in compounding rates become very sensitive over the long term.

The first thing to determine is the definition of long term. The famous British economist John Maynard Keynes argued that since in the long term we are all dead, the definition of long term is roughly similar to life expectancy and can be defined as 75 years. However the life of each generation is a short period in history for institutional investors, endowments, sovereign funds and family offices. This group of investors should therefore think in terms of several generations as being the definition of long term.

Compounding investment returns over 75 years clearly demonstrates the effect that apparently small differences in rates has on total returns. The table below shows the result of four annual compounding rates applied to an initial investment of $1,000.

Compounding Rate	Future Value	Investment Multiple	Illustrative Returns
5% per annum	$38,833	39 times	Money Market Returns
10% per annum	$1,271,895	1,272 times	Lower Quartile Active Equity Returns
12% per annum	$4,913,056	4,913 times	Median Active Equity Returns
15% per annum	$35,672,868	35,673 times	All World Index Returns

Table 7: Compounding Rates on $1,000 over 75 years

An investor happy to accept a net money market benchmark of 5% in an accumulation fund for 75 years will increase the value of his initial $1,000 investment to $38,833 over 75 years, a multiple of nearly 39 times. A net equity return (after all costs) of 10% increases the multiple to 1,272 times. An investor's sweet spot tends to starts at around 10% per annum and every increment thereafter is highly significant. Finding a way to increase the net performance of the investment either by increasing returns or by saving additional costs of 2% per annum results in a multiple of 4,913 times, over 3.5 times as much as a 10% return. If you achieving a net return of 15%, it's a spectacular achievement, nearly 1,000 times better than money market returns, with a multiple of 35,673 times.

You have probably already noticed that the investment multiples shown above demonstrate a geometric relationship between the compounding rate and the multiple achieved. That's why compounding rates of over 15% per annum produces some truly startling results. One investor who has achieved a compound return of over 22% for over 30 years is Warren Buffett, judged to be the richest man in the world. Check these numbers in your calculator. If his firm Berkshire Hathaway maintains a 22% per annum track record for 75 years, the investment multiple would be 3 million times the original sum invested. Some sweet spot.

Appreciating the above table is one of the greatest secrets of successful investment management. Our interpretation is that your long term results reflect four factors:

1. **The Choice of Reference Index**

   A theoretical world index of all the listed companies in existence describes what economists call a zero sum game, open to all investors. By owning some but not all shares in the world index, your performance can be a little higher or a little lower than the world index, but all investors, measured together would see their profits and losses even out. The global result, by definition, is that disregarding any transaction costs or taxes, all investors must make the same return as the world index. Unfortunately, transaction costs and taxes turn global investments into a negative sum game: all investors, measured together, will make a return that is marginally less than the world index return.

   Very few investors invest in a world index. Because the liabilities of their funds are in $, most US investors benchmark themselves against the S&P 500 or the Wilshire 5,000 indices. Similarly, most UK investors benchmark themselves against the FTSE All-Share Index and so on. When choosing an index fund there is no right or wrong answer but any divergence from the world index means that returns will diverge from the world result, perhaps up, perhaps down.

   The most important asset allocation decision you face is the choice of an Islamic benchmark or the selection of a range of Islamic benchmarks that best address the objectives and liabilities of your fund. Because it is representative, we recommend the FTSE Shariah All World $ Index as the default benchmark for all Islamic investors.

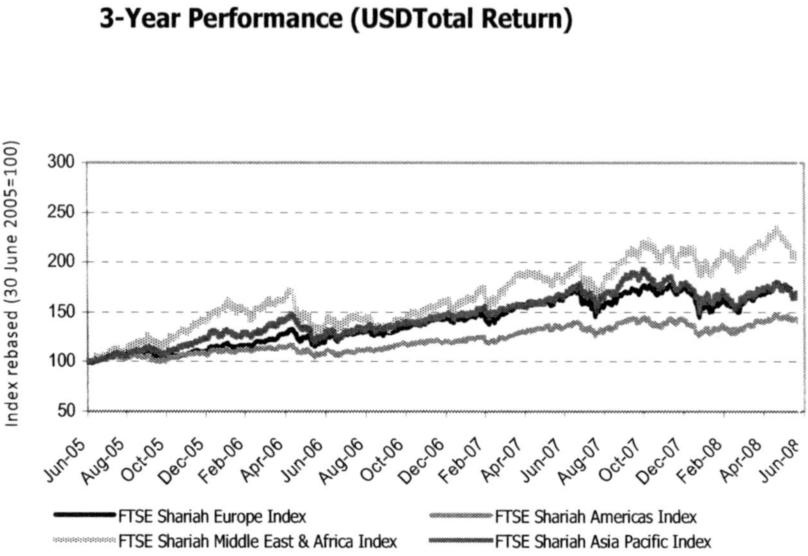

3-Year Performance (USDTotal Return)

Source: FTSE Group, as at 30 June 2008. Shariah indices are based on back tests.

Figure 41: 3 year performance of FTSE Shariah All-World index versus FTSE All-World Index

As shown in the above graph, some divergence between the FTSE Shariah All World index and the conventional FTSE All World index is inevitable, as their constituents are not the same. The reason why the relative performance of the Sharia'a index has produced a higher return is that the companies it excludes are in sectors that have underperformed during the review period.

2. The Expense Ratio of Running a Fund

The costs of running a fund are a mix of fund transaction fees, fund management fees and taxes. Active fund management fees can add an extra 1% to 2% to the expense ratio. In addition, fees may be payable when joining or leaving a fund, and capital gain tax or stamp duty may be required when the fund buys and sells shares. When funds receive dividends, they may be subject to withholding taxes and transaction charges.

These costs, which could accumulate to more than 2% per annum, penalise performance creating a significant drag on long term performance. Minimising the total expense ratio of a fund is an important job of a fund manager.

Conventional index funds recover an element of their expenses (around 25 basis points per annum) by a technique called stock lending. Conventional index funds lend stocks against cash collateral to hedge funds and receive a stock lending fee in return. Hedge funds can then sell the stock they have borrowed to create short positions. Sharia'a law does not permit short selling, and this technique can not be applied.

3. **The Stock Turnover within a Fund**

If an active equity fund has a stock turnover of 80% per annum, it means that only 20% of the shares held at the end of a year are the same as the shares that were held at the beginning of the year. Discounts to mid-market prices, broker's commissions and taxes add to the expense ratio as stock turnover increases. This explains why highly active stock managers have to make very good decisions if their stock selection decisions are to add value for the investor.

In comparison, changes of index composition mean that the average stock turnover within a partially replicated index fund is around 5% per annum. Otherwise stock turnover in an index fund is only a function of new buyers (net of sellers) and switching.

4. **Timing Differences caused by Cash and Dividends.**

Holding cash in a fund from new subscriptions and dividends causes an investment lag against index performance. Since an index fund usually owns a large number of shares, dealing in all of the shares every time there is a new subscription would be uneconomic. Conventional index funds manage this process (as well as the process of changing index composition) by partial replication methods (or "sampling") and by investing in derivatives.

Derivatives and options are not permitted for *sharia'a* compliant funds and can not be used to manage portfolio changes and cash balances. For this reason, Islamic index funds may have slightly higher tracking errors than conventional index funds.

In summary, we believe maximising compound returns over the long term is the secret of investment success. Unfortunately, the tyranny of compound costs is the reason why the net performance of nearly all funds falls below benchmark returns.

Over the medium and long term, index funds will outperform nearly all active funds because their costs are less. This is the simple but compelling competitive advantage of index funds. Most active fund managers can not recover this simple competitive advantage through superior investment analysis and stock picking. In addition, the main issue facing investors when selecting active fund managers is that historic out-performance is not a particularly good indicator of future out-performance. Too often, yesterday's star performer is tomorrow's under achiever.

11.3.3 Secret 2: Sharia'a Compliant Indices Outperform Conventional Indices

As becomes apparent from the graph in figure 42, the FTSE Shariah All World $ Index outperformed its conventional benchmark by over 10% in the year to June 2008. More generally, FTSE Shariah indices outperformed conventional reference indices in all 12 cases summarised above. This is another little-known secret and a major competitive advantage for all investors, whether Islamic or not.

In addition, you can see that the recent performance (over the last three years) of the FTSE Shariah Emerging $ Index has been extraordinary and at 30% per annum compound appears to be unsustainable in the medium to long term.

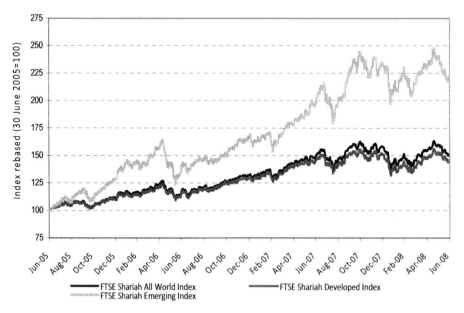

3-Year Performance (USD Total Return)

Source: FTSE Group, as at 30 June 2008. Sharia'a indices are based on back tests.

Figure 42: 3 year performance of FTSE Shariah Indices

However, we believe there are good arguments to suggest the relative out-performance of emerging markets may continue (including the out-performance of individual developing markets like MENA within this global category).

11.3.4 Secret 3: *Sharia'a* Indices are Liquid

A third secret is that, like their conventional counterparts, the above Islamic indices have large market capitalisations and are therefore naturally liquid. Scale and liquidity should not be constraints for investors deciding to switch their core equity asset allocations into equity trackers based on the above FTSE Shariah indices.

Index Constituents as at 30 June 2008

Index	Number of Stocks	Market Capitalisation ($trillion)
FTSE Shariah All World $ Index	1,406	15.9
FTSE All World $ Index	2,916	29.9
FTSE Shariah Emerging $ Index	444	2.2
FTSE Emerging $ Index	914	3.6
FTSE Shariah Developed $ Index	962	13.6
FTSE Developed $ Index	2,002	26.3

Table 8: Index constituents

The FTSE Shariah All World Index can be broken down into regional indices, including:

Selection of FTSE Shariah Regional Indices as at 30 June 2008

Index	Number of Stocks	Market Capitalisation ($trillion)
FTSE Shariah Developed Europe	223	4.3
FTSE Shariah Developed Asia Pacific	419	2.4
FTSE Shariah Developed Americas	380	7.5
FTSE Shariah Middle East & Africa	59	0.3
FTSE Shariah China	60	0.1
FTSE Shariah India	55	0.1

Table 9: Selection of FTSE Shariah Regional Indices

It is worth noting the liquidity of some of these indices is still measured in the hundreds of billions rather than trillions and the recent performance of the first four of these is set out below.

3-Year Performance (USD Total Return)

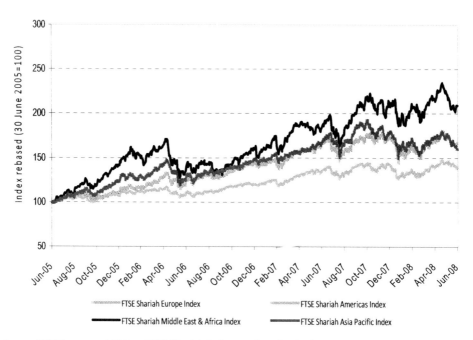

Source: FTSE Group, as at 30 June 2008. Sharia'a indices are based on back tests.

Figure 43: 3 year performance of FTSE Shariah Indices

11.3.5 Secret 4 - How Islamic Money Market Assets Can Avoid Interest

Our simple asset allocation model suggests that an Islamic fund with limited short term liabilities should hold around 20% of its assets in cash to avoid any unnecessary risks and volatility when meeting its obligations.

Cash investments that earn interest are abhorrent to Sharia'a law but currency investments that do not make any investment return are unnecessarily inefficient. We suggest Islamic investors make use of Sharia'a compliant money market assets with an appropriate mix of liquidity, security and return.

The following money market assets can be used to generate a return on liquid assets:

1. Commodity *Murabaha*
2. *Ijara*
3. *Sukuk*
4. *Wakala*
5. *Sharia'a* Compliant Money Market Funds

For the instruments mentioned under points 1 – 4 see chapter 4 for a more detailed description. In addition, Islamic Money Market funds can also invest in other *sharia'a* compliant money market funds.

Because many Islamic treasury products (such as commodity *murabaha*) are for fixed terms and can not be broken, the maturity profile of the money market instruments will be carefully managed to ensure an optimum liquidity profile without having to keep a significant amount of the funds in cash.

11.3.6 Our Recommendations

As set out above, our simple asset allocation model for an Islamic fund with limited short term liabilities is 60% in core index funds, 20% in satellite funds and 20% in cash. On this basis, investors need a "core" fund for 80% of any Islamic investment portfolio, with satellites outsourced to selected managers.

Our first secret was to show how sensitive long term investment performance is to apparently small changes in compound rates of return. We suggested the sweet spot for investors starts at 10% per annum and for years you could have comfortably achieved this by investing in index funds.

Our second secret suggests you could have achieved better than average results by simply switching out of conventional index funds into liquid Sharia'a compliant index funds.

Our third secret was to show you can get well into the sweet spot by tracking the FTSE Shariah All World $ Index which for the last three years has returned 14.75% per annum.

Our fourth secret was that for the last three years, tracking the FTSE Shariah Emerging Markets $ Index was up in Berkshire Hathaway territory with a compound return of 30% per annum. Mr Buffet would probably point out that three years is only a short period for intelligent investors.

In summary, based on the last five years, we recommend you should invest in a fund that tracks the FTSE Shariah All World Index and the FTSE Shariah Emerging Markets Index, with less exposure to the developed world, particularly the USA.

ASSET MANAGEMENT

Our final secret was that returns from money market assets can be optimised using the Sharia'a compliant products contained in a suitable fund. This facility completes the puzzle for investors wanting to manage their core asset allocations in a compliant way.

12 Risks in Islamic Banks

The ethical framework governing Islamic Finance prohibits gambling, uncertainty and interest. Although at first glance this sounds like a risk manager's dream, it does not at all mean that an Islamic bank runs little to no risk. Like other banks and financial institutions, Islamic banks face risks inherent to the financial industry, and in most countries they have to abide by the same rules as other financial institutions for the calculation of regulatory capital. However, Islamic banks also have their own set of unique risk management challenges.

Conventional banks are subject to a wide range of risks which are described in table 10 below.

Type of Risk	Description
Liquidity Risk	The risk of insufficient liquidity for normal operating requirements, that is the ability of the bank to meet its liabilities when they fall due
Interest Rate Risk	The risk arising from interest rate mismatches in volume, maturity and type (fixed vs. floating) of interest-sensitive assets, liabilities and off-balance sheet items
Credit Risk	The risk that an asset or a loan becomes irrecoverable in the case of outright default, or the risk of delay in the servicing of the loan
Settlement or counterparty Risk	The risk that occurs if one party to a transaction pays funds or delivers assets prior to receiving its own funds or assets, hence exposing it to a potential loss
Price Risk	The risk that the market price of an instrument traded in a well-defined market will be volatile. Market risk occurs in relation to debt securities, derivatives, equity derivatives and currency transactions held by a bank
Leverage Risk (Capital Adequacy)	The risk related to the extent to which the assets of a bank may decline before the positions of its depositors and other creditors are jeopardised
Event or Operational Risk	The risk of certain events occurring, e.g. disaster, regulatory or political events, or the (temporary) unavailability of IT systems
Business Risk	The risks related to products, macro-economic cycles and technology changes

Table 10: Types of risks for conventional banks

The need to quantify these risks has resulted in the development of what is currently the most widely used risk measure for banks, Value at Risk (VaR). VaR attempts to measure the downside risk of either a portfolio or, in aggregation, a firm into one single number, taking into account financial leverage and diversification effects. The result of the VaR equation is represented in the maximum amount a bank is likely to stand to lose on a given day or over a number of days (e.g. over a period of one week), generally with a confidence interval of 95% or 99%. It incorporates traditional risks and risks related to adverse market movements of financial derivatives and structured products. In addition, VaR may also be used as a basis for calculating the amount of economic capital required to support a business, which is an essential component of economic value added measures. VaR mainly provides an indication of the maximum risk a bank is exposed to under predictive conditions (e.g. the assumption that the distribution of the underlying price data is approximately normal), and may not necessarily be suitable as an internal measure to control risk or to determine profitability. VaR is, for instance, used in the calculation of regulatory capital required to support market risk under the Basel Capital Accords. Besides VaR, Risk Adjusted Return on Capital (RAROC) is often used as a risk measure by banks. The purpose of RAROC is to adjust trading profits by the remuneration of risk capital, and it recognises that trading positions with a higher risk profile require a larger amount of economic capital to absorb larger potential losses.

Any risk taken by a bank will have to be evaluated against its risk management system, as well as the cost of the measures in place. The complexity of banks seriously hinders simple assessment of the risks taken and how they are controlled. However, it will not be possible to incorporate safeguards against all risks within the risk management system of a bank. A more complex risk management system may actually make the situation worse, due to the increasing complexity that is introduced.

The absence of interest, and hence of interest rate risk as such, does not imply that an Islamic bank can be considered to bear lower levels of risk. Like conventional banks, Islamic banks incur liquidity, credit, settlement, leverage, operational and business risk. In addition different types of risk can be identified for Islamic banks in the form of changes in asset and liability returns and value, due to changing economic circumstances affecting the investments that are part of the portfolio of the bank. Instead of fixed-rate interest rate risk, which is a balance sheet (fair value) exposure, Islamic banks face a rate of return risk, which is an income statement (cash flow) exposure, similar in nature to floating-rate interest rate risk in conventional banks. Rate of return risk is mainly related to sale-based instruments such as *murabaha, salam*, and *istisna* as well as *ijara* instruments. Although the risks are considered to be small for short term *murabaha* contracts, the risk increases for transactions with a longer maturity. One of the risk mitigation techniques in use is to link *ijara* rentals to a benchmark such as LIBOR or an inflation index and periodically adjust the rental amounts.

In order to measure the risk of an Islamic bank properly, the applicable conventional bank risks need to be taken into consideration, and complemented by additional risk types that cater specifically for the risks undertaken by Islamic banks such as[25]:

Fiduciary Risk. Specifically, risk related to the nature of the *mudaraba* contract, which places liability for losses on the *mudarib* (or agent) in the case of malfeasance, negligence or breach of contract on the part of the management of the *mudaraba*.

Displaced Commercial Risk. This risk type is related to the common practice among Islamic banks to "smooth" the financial returns to investment account holders by varying the percentage of profit taken as the *mudarib* share, which can be compared to an arrangement or agency fee.

Rate of Return Risk. The risk of a mismatch between yields on assets and the expected rates of both restricted and unrestricted investment accounts which may in turn lead to Displaced Commercial Risk

Generally, the differences between the operations of conventional and Islamic banks result in a different level of risk on the bank as a whole. Riskiness of Islamic banks is perceived to be higher than conventional banks, for instance due to the profit and loss sharing modes of financing and the related increased potential for moral hazard, the potential incentive for risk taking without adequate capital levels, the lower levels of risk-hedging instruments and techniques, and underdeveloped or nonexistent capital markets. A significant part of the higher perceived risk levels is, however, associated with the fact that most Islamic banks are based in jurisdictions that are considered to be emerging markets. With Islamic finance gaining popularity in the Western world, more banks are starting to operate out of financial centres such as London. These institutions need to be authorised and regulated by Western financial regulators and will have to compete in a rounded financial environment. The risk levels of these banks is not higher than that of their conventional counterparts, and could even be considered lower due to the absence of speculative instruments that has caused such large disruption in the financial markets around the end of 2007 and has an ongoing impact on the global economy.

---

[25] Archer, S., and R.A.A. Karim (2006) *On Capital Structure, Risk Sharing and Capital Adequacy in Islamic Banks,* International Journal of Theoretical and Applied Finance, Vol. 9, No. 3 (2006) 269-280

13 *Sharia'a* Supervisory Board

Contributed by Abdulkhaliq Elshayyal

Despite the universality of Islamic finance, the underlying principles of it are religion based. This creates an inherent requirement for Islamic financial structures, products and transactions to be *sharia'a* compliant. This requirement, apart from fulfilling the specific religious conditions, meets two principal demands. The first emerges from the financial institutions' viewpoint, who need to ensure that the product and services they offer are genuinely *sharia'a* compliant and thus in line with the institutions' standards, principles and shareholders' requirement, and the second from the investors' and clients' perspective, in guaranteeing that their investments are in line with *sharia'a*.

With the growth of both stand alone Islamic banks (also referred to as *sharia'a* based) and Islamic windows (or *sharia'a* compliant) offering Islamic financial services as well as specialist Islamic financial institutions (mainly investment companies and funds), the role of the *Sharia'a* Supervisory Board (SSB) has developed and become more noticeable. Initially, it was common practice to turn to Muslim scholars specialising in Islamic law and jurisprudence and with a background in finance who would advise the institution on the traditional products being offered and approve the product as a financial instrument. Increasingly, scholars became more involved in advising on and structuring more innovative products and adaptations of more conventional products with *sharia'a* principles which were now being sought in the Islamic finance industry. With the development of the industry, more attention is given to the scholars and the SSBs they sat on as their roles advanced into less orthodox areas.

In order to obtain a full understanding of the roles and responsibilities of the SSB, this chapter will provide a review of their different functions, analyse the mechanics of selecting the SSB, discuss the governance issues surrounding the SSB and finally look at the challenges facing them.

13.1 Roles

The roles and functions of the SSB can be divided into three main areas; the advisory role, the approval role and the audit role. Whilst operating in these areas, the board must conform to set guidelines of Islamic jurisprudence as well as taking into consideration industry standards such as the AAOIFI standards mentioned in chapter 14.1.5 when required.

13.1.1 The Advisory Role

Often Islamic banks require clarification and opinions on specific matters which are covered by *sharia'a* principles. Here, the SSB will advise on such specific matters, as well as more generic issues that arise. Due to the nature of the businesses and industry elements, best practice would be for institutions offering Islamic financial services to maintain an in-house *sharia'a* specialist or an employee with in-depth knowledge of *sharia'a* teachings. This would not only enhance the knowledge available within the institution, but generally also improve the effectiveness of the SSB since issues can in the first instance be referred to the in-house specialist and thus achieving maximum utilisation of the SSB while productively managing resources. This is also a recommendation made by AAOIFI and as such should ideally be adhered to by Islamic financial institutions.

13.1.2 The Approval Role

The SSB approval process spans several steps. The SSB first reviews the initial structures and concepts to ensure they are in line with *sharia'a* and once approval is obtained, and the product is structured, further approval is required in light of the legal documentation required. This process can extend to several revisions depending on the transaction and the legal and SSB requirements. Final approval is also required for specific transactions where the structures are highly individual in nature and for more complex structures e.g. syndications. Figure 44 illustrates best practice for *sharia'a* support.

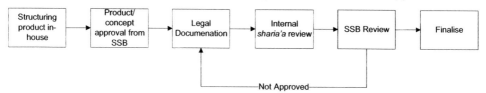

Figure 44: *Sharia'a* approval process for a new product or structure

The process outlined above, is a generic process and can differ on a transaction by transaction basis.

It is also worth bearing in mind that approval for a structure does not automatically equate to approval of the documentation of the structure. For example, the SSB may approve a certain product as *sharia'a* compliant based on the concepts and their understanding of the structure. However, this does not imply that the documentation of the structure has been approved. Thus, institutions issuing such *fatawa* should remain diligent so as to ensure approval is obtained on the final structure as well as the documentation.

The process for changes to an existing structure that has previously been approved is shorter and is depicted in Figure 45 below.

Figure 45: *Sharia'a* approval process for changes to an existing product or structure

13.1.3 The Audit Role

It is the responsibility of the SSB to ensure ex-post compliance by verifying that transactions which have been entered into by the Islamic financial institution which are certified as *sharia'a* compliant have in fact complied with the SSB guidelines and associated *fatawa*.

This two pronged approach in ensuring compliance is in line with the SSB operational and governance standards in certifying full *sharia'a* compliance of the Islamic financial institution and extends to institutions' day-to-day operations. Leading on from this, the SSB also has an important duty in performing a *sharia'a* audit on the institution. In this case, the SSB does not only operate as an ex-post compliance medium but also satisfies the shareholders of the institution. The audit process varies from institution to institution but is generally done on the basis of a departmental audit. The regularity of the SSB audit also varies and depends mainly on size of the institution and the number of transactions they execute. The audit can take place annually, semi annually or quarterly. Part of the SSB audit and control function is also the calculation of *zakat* obligations. Depending on the institution and local regulations, *zakat* contributions are either made by the institution or delegated to the individual shareholders. Either way, the SSB has to provide calculations of the *zakat* obligations on a per share basis.

13.2 Social Responsibilities

In adopting its rules and duties, the SSB is not only fulfilling its functions within the financial institution but also adhering to the wider responsibility which it bears in implementing Islamic structures in a social sense. Ethical behaviour and *sharia'a* compliance are the responsibility of the SSB members and by fulfilling their role in a financial institution and the industry in general, SSB members are seen to perform a wider religious obligation.

SSB members contribute to the development of the industry through the development of products and the implementation of *sharia'a* rules and guidelines on both exiting and more contemporary products, and are valuable contributors to the progress of the industry. Their role here is unique in that they are well placed at the centre of the developments of and debate in the industry as shown in Figure 46.

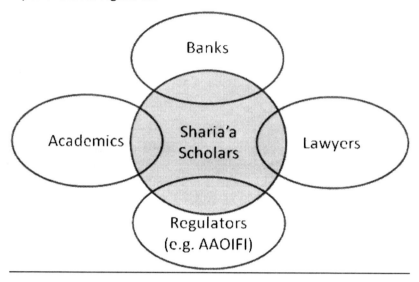

Figure 46 - Role of the SSB within the industry

As *zakat* is regarded as a mechanism of wealth purification and income redistribution in Islam, the SSB's role in calculating zakat payable by the institutions shareholders is also regarded as a social responsibility for the greater benefit of the society. This method of wealth redistribution is not only seen as a fulfilment of one of the major religious principles but also as a method of purification for the institution. The SSB will also ensure and supervise that any penalty payments paid to the institution are directed to a charity or scientific or educational cause. This will also be the case with any non-*sharia'a* compliant revenue.

SSBs also have the responsibility of maintaining confidence in the institution. Reputational risk is an important aspect in the financial industry and equally so among Islamic financial institutions and the opinions and advice of the SSB are clearly mentioned and relied upon. Thus, shareholders rely on SSB decisions and it is the duty of the scholars to ensure that they maintain the bank's reputation through maintaining best practice.

13.3 Corporate Governance

Like conventional financial institutions, Islamic financial institutions typically have the same governance structure which is made up of a more senior, or supervisory board, chaired by the chairman of the company and a lower board, or Executive Committee, responsible for the day-to-day running of the bank. Remuneration committees, audit committees and risk committees are all standard components of the governance structure. However, in addition to all the usual committees, Islamic financial institutions have an additional organ of governance in the SSB. Due to the dualistic nature of Islamic financial institutions in that they have to follow both financial and *sharia'a* regulations, and national regulation e.g. the FSA, Islamic financial institutions are subject to a unique corporate governance structure. Five main elements are generally identified when considering the SSB role in the governance structure:

- **Independence.** Independence of the SSB and SSB members is a fundamental requirement and is an issue which is frequently discussed and debated. In order for an SSB to function effectively, its members must be independent from the management of the bank. As a result, the SSB members are usually appointed by the shareholders at the AGM.

- **Confidentiality.** Due to the nature of the SSB members' work and duties, they are exposed to a great amount of proprietary information. Their presence, as is common, on many boards dictates a detailed confidentiality requirement.

- **Competence.** Due to the multifaceted nature of the SSB members' role, the SSB members are required to have a specialist knowledge and expertise. Not only are they expected to have a specialist *sharia'a* knowledge and expertise and in particular *fiqh al muamalat* (Islamic law of contracts) but also an understanding and knowledge of modern financial and banking practices and products.

- **Consistence.** The SSB should also remain consistent in their decisions, guidelines and advice in order to build up and maintain consumer confidence. This is an important requirement and is mutually beneficial for both the client and the bank.

- **Disclosure.** Disclosure and transparency are a vital part of the SSB roles and functions. By disclosing procedures, decisions, *fatawa* and structural details, the SSB encourages and promotes confidence not only for shareholders but also the industry and the wider public.

All the above elements are an integral part of their work as the industry grows and shows the instrumental nature of the SSB within the organisation.

13.4 Structures and variations of *Sharia'a* Supervisory Boards

Due to the various needs and the differing nature of both Islamic and conventional financial institutions requiring *sharia'a* compliance, there are similar alternative structures to SSBs as well as certain factors which should be considered when selecting SSB members. Although there is not much substantive difference of opinion between the main schools of thought in Islam when it comes to principles of Islamic finance, many Muslims tend to follow a certain school of thought in their day-to-day practice of the religion and consequently extend this following to specific financial transactions. As such, they would prefer to invest in certain products which have been Islamically approved by a scholar who adheres to their particular school of thought. This is particularly apparent in certain countries where, incidentally, the Muslim population of such countries generally belongs to a particular school of thought, for example the Shafi'is in Malaysia and the Hanafis in Pakistan. Thus, in Malaysia for example, investors might require approval by a Shafi'i scholar before investing in a certain transaction and similarly in Saudi Arabia, an investor may decide not to invest in a the same product if it has not been approved by a Hanbali scholar. In order to overcome this hurdle, and to provide comfort to their clients and investors, institutions tend to select SSB members from each school of thought. This provides such clients with the added reassurance they require, knowing that any product offered to them by the institution would have been certified as *sharia'a* compliant by a scholar from their school of thought.

The presence of certain scholars on several boards inevitably leads to the difficulty of obtaining the same level of service from all scholars. Thus, when selecting members of the SSB it is also important to remember commitments of the scholars and accessibility to them. This plays a vital role in developing relations with scholars and increases the long term value added to the institutions if planned effectively. This accessibility to the scholars is an area which should be carefully considered before hand as this will also greatly enhance the resources of the institution.

Today, these factors have been adopted in contrasting ways and have generally proved to be successful in meeting their objectives. In overcoming the challenge of providing approval from certain scholars, some institutions have opted for creating regional SSBs comprised of regional scholars prevalent in those regions whilst simultaneously appointing a central SSB with a member from each school of thought. Other banks operating in a single jurisdiction have chosen to appoint a single scholar (at times exclusive to the institution) who is highly respected and reputable in the country of operation and thus also obtaining unparalleled access to him. Alternatively, in order to achieve a similar level of frequent access, certain institutions have decided to appoint local scholars to their SSBs as opposed to more well known and experienced scholars who may not be able to provide the same level of time and attention which the institution may require. This also provides such scholars, who are mostly less known, with a platform to the industry.

Another approach taken by some institutions is to create within their SSBs a further executive committee. This would usually be composed of two members who would have the additional responsibility of acting on behalf of the SSB on urgent matters and assume delegation on certain issues. The executive committee would generally contain the chairman of the SSB.

Although, the AAOIFI standard on the appointment of the members of the SSB for Islamic financial institutions, requires the SSB to have a minimum of three members, as discussed this is not always the case in practice. Having said that, there does not appear to be any substantive conflict between the AAOIFI standard and the alternative approaches adopted with regards the number of members on SSBs as these institutions which opt for less than three members do so for specific reasons, be it the level of business is sufficient to be covered by less than three scholars or they are in the process of expansion or they are subject to a higher supervisory board.

13.5 Challenges facing *Sharia'a* Supervisory Boards

As discussed earlier, the levels of competence of scholars required to fulfil the roles and functions of the SSB are high. As a result, scholars who are in the unique position of combining an understanding of *sharia'a* principles and *fiqh al muamalat* together with knowledge of financial products and services are highly sought after. This has naturally led to the presence of the same highly qualified scholars on several SSBs. Although this has been raised frequently as a criticism of scholars and as a shortcoming of the industry, it is important to bear in mind several reasons for this. The experience of the scholars in their roles as *sharia'a* advisors for banks and financial institutions has ultimately fuelled the industry's demand for them and as a result they have met this demand. Furthermore the high level and specialist nature of their position is not easily met and consequently the lack of resources available in the industry and in specific lack of experienced professionals is a main challenge. This is mainly at a practitioner level, so whilst there are many academics and commentators on Islamic finance and related issues, the industry in terms of bankers, lawyers, accountants is in great demand for experienced professionals with a strong understanding of Islamic finance and the principles it is based on. Although, recent initiatives have been set up to fill this gap such as the AAOIFI *sharia'a* advisor and audit qualification, further work is needed in order to ensure that as the industry continues to grow through these current conditions, this growth is led and contributed to by specialists with the background in as well as the vision for the success of the industry whilst not departing from its underlying foundations and purpose. This is a collective responsibility of the industry to promote and maintain best practice. However the *sharia'a* scholars in particular have a specific role here in terms of guidance and advice through their position in the industry as discussed earlier. The SII has also launched an initiative to develop scholars' knowledge of the financial industry. As discussed, this knowledge is an important tool for the scholars in order to keep track of current developments in the wider industry.

As the industry continues to grow at an unprecedented rate, the opportunity for development and innovation has also increased. Naturally, this has led to different approaches in different areas of the industry on the same issues. Together with the geographical and religious factors, this multiple approach to single issues has created a noticeable inconsistency in the market which has been frequently debated and commented on. Although efforts towards achieving harmonisation have a strong basis and foundation in the AAOIFI *sharia'a* standards, further uniformity is required bearing in mind the size of the industry and the need for sustained growth based on a [consistent] model. More recent schemes such as the IIFM-produced Master Agreement for Treasury Placement are instrumental in achieving this uniformity.

To conclude, SSBs do not only play a central role in the governance and development of Islamic financial institutions, they have been essential and critical to the expansion of the industry as a whole and the continued innovation which is developing in it. Although different approaches and models have been adopted by various institutions as a means of achieving and ensuring *sharia'a* compliance through SSBs, the underlying principle remains the same across the board and whilst the need for greater harmonisation and uniformity is required, it is important to bear in mind that the inherent nature of the *sharia'a* provides for difference of opinion and disagreement.

14 The Islamic Financial Infrastructure

Islamic financial institutions generally operate within the conventional regulatory environment, in some cases with additional regulation that caters to the specifics of the Islamic financial industry. Although different regulatory and advisory bodies govern the workings of Islamic financial institutions, this does not mean that their regulations are mandatory in every jurisdiction. The remainder of this chapter reviews how Islamic financial institutions are regulated, additional regulatory bodies and some of the lesser known types of institutions in the Islamic financial market place. Finally, a short note on why LIBOR is suitable as a benchmark when determining the profit margin on an Islamic financial transaction.

14.1 Regulatory Institutions

Besides financial regulators, there are four main institutions that are directly associated with Islamic Finance, each of which is explored in more detail here.

14.1.1 Financial Regulators

Generally Islamic financial institutions are regulated in a similar way to other financial institutions, although the application varies from country to country. Three different models for financial regulation can generally be observed in the market:

1. **Fully Islamic.** In this model, all financial institutions operating in a country are fully Islamic, and no conventional financial institutions are authorised to operate. A fully Islamic financial system is, for instance, operational in Iran.

2. **Dual Regulation.** In this case, both conventional and Islamic financial institutions operate in a country, and they are typically authorised and regulated by the same financial regulator, but using a different set of regulations for each. The separation of regulatory environment recognises the fact that there are differences between conventional and Islamic institutions and allows the regulator to take Islamic bank specifics into consideration. This does not, however, imply that there are two distinct organisations for conventional and Islamic financial institutions. The regulatory body is typically the same organisation. Dual regulation is, for instance, operational in Malaysia and Bahrain.

3. **Single Regulation.** In this case, Islamic banks are regulated by the same regulator applying the same regulations that apply to conventional banks.

This is for instance the case in the UK where the regulator works on the basis of "no obstacles, no special favours", resulting in a situation that regulations equally apply across all types of institutions.

14.1.2 The *Fiqh* Academy

Fiqh is the Arabic word used to indicate the understanding or interpretation of *sharia'a* and is generally used to represent the opinion of scholars trained in Islamic jurisprudence. Based in Jeddah, the Islamic *fiqh* academy was established to provide a uniform view of the permissibility of Islamic financial products. Although individual scholars still have different views on the acceptability of individual transactions, the academy's rulings are well respected by the majority of scholars and *sharia'a* supervisory board members.

14.1.3 Islamic Development Bank

The Islamic Development Bank (IDB) became operational in 1975 and is based in Jeddah with the remit to organise funding for projects in member countries. The IDB raises funds from other Islamic institutions to fund the projects, and often works closely together with development assistance agencies such as the World Bank.

14.1.4 Islamic Financial Services Board

The Islamic Financial Services Board (IFSB) was established in Malaysia in 2002 and advises regulators on how Islamic financial institutions should be managed. The IFSB provides guidelines for capital adequacy, risk management and corporate governance for Islamic Financial Institutions which regulators can adopt. The financial regulators in Malaysia and Bahrain, for instance, have largely adopted the capital adequacy guidelines for Islamic banks.

IFSB members are global regulators and other market participants, and new guidelines and best practices are developed continuously.

14.1.5 Accounting and Auditing Organisation for Islamic Financial Institutions

The Accounting and Auditing Organisation for Islamic Financial Institutions is based in Bahrain and is responsible for the development of accounting, auditing and *sharia'a* standards. The AAOIFI standards are largely based on the international financial reporting standards (IFRS) and prescribe additional guidelines for Islamic financial institutions where the IFRS standards do not sufficiently reflect the specifics of Islamic finance.

AAOIFI standards are mandatory in some countries and are used in others as guidelines. Western Islamic financial institutions, however, are generally obliged to apply IFRS and can chose to also present their financial reports in accordance with AAOIFI standards, but this is on a voluntary basis.

14.1.6 International Islamic Financial Markets

The International Islamic Financial Markets (IIFM) is established in Bahrain with the support of the central banks of Bahrain, Brunei, Indonesia, Sudan and the Islamic Development Banks. The IIFM's mandate is to take part in the establishment, development, self-regulation and promotion of an Islamic Capital and Money Market. IIFM is working on initiatives with ISDA and ICMA to develop Islamic financial master agreements and is working with on standardisation of contracts within the industry.

14.2 Socially Responsible Investments and Micro Finance

Both socially responsible investing and micro-finance fit very well within the Islamic finance framework due to their focus on social responsibility and wealth distribution.

14.2.1 Socially Responsible Investments

Socially responsible investing, also known as sustainable or ethical investing, encompasses an investment strategy that seeks to maximise both financial return and socially responsible or ethical behaviour. Faith and conscience are probably the most important factors for people to make ethical investment decisions, and generally, socially responsible investors favour investments that promote environmental stewardship, consumer protection, human rights and diversity. In addition, some investors actively avoid investing in any businesses that are involved with alcohol, tobacco, gambling, and weaponry and defence. Due to the prohibitions in *sharia'a,* Islamic investments avoid the following industries:

- **Conventional Banking and Insurance.** Conventional banking and insurance is associated with interest and is therefore not permissible.

- **Alcohol and alcohol production.** This includes any distilling, marketing and sales activities.

- **Pork related products and non-compliant food production.** Non-compliant food production covers everything which is not prepared in a *halal* way and covers, among others, meat which is not slaughtered in an acceptable fashion.

- **Gambling.** This covers casinos and betting shops, but also bingo halls and on-line betting

- **Tobacco.** As with alcohol, this includes the production, marketing and sales of tobacco and associated products.

- **Adult entertainment.** Any activity associated with adult entertainment including escort services, brothels and movies with explicit sexual content.

- **Weapons, arms and defence manufacturing.**

In addition, highly leveraged investments are also avoided since these generally involve an element of interest income or payment.

Besides the prohibitions on certain industries, interest, gambling and uncertainty, *sharia'a* there are other elements that make *sharia'a* investing fit well with ethical investments. *Sharia'a* acknowledges the right of an individual to create wealth, but discourages hoarding, monopolistic activities and excessive materialism. In addition, *sharia'a* encourages social justices without hampering entrepreneurship.

Although the industries individual investors wish to avoid will depend on their individual preference and view on ethical investments, the principles of *sharia'a* generally sit very well with non-Muslim investors seeking socially responsible investment opportunities and offer a viable alternative to other opportunities available in the market.

14.2.2 Micro Finance

By its nature, Islamic finance is very suitable for micro financing type projects. The investments are typically in a tangible business venue and have a high level of social responsibility attached to them.

There is a wide range of structures in Islamic finance that lends itself to micro finance initiatives, with the partnership contracts such as *musharaka* and *mudaraba* potentially the most suitable. Micro financiers tend to have a very close relationship with their clients, which makes a partnership ultimately viable. The bank will not only supply money, but also expertise related to the setting up and successful running of a company. It is highly likely that the client will initially only put in expertise and will take their profit share. However, from experience with conventional micro finance, it appears that the entrepreneurs are likely to want to obtain full ownership over their business which could become a feature of the contract. Looking at a $100 investment, a suggested structure could be as follows:

- Bank invests $100 and receives 40% of the profit for their input of both capital and expertise

- 20% of the profit is held by the bank in a savings account which can be used as a buffer for unforeseen circumstances or to purchase units in the partnership from the bank

- 40% of the profit is paid directly to the entrepreneur.

The advantage of this is that it provides a form of security to the entrepreneur and encourages savings to be built up. The entrepreneur should, however, be free to use other funds (e.g. excess profits) to repurchase units.

In The Middle East and Asia entrepreneurial loans on this scale are often granted on an informal basis by small groups of friends, neighbours and family. The intensive nature of micro finance in combination with the fact that clients typically are not deemed credit worthy and the subsequent additional capital charge does not necessarily make micro finance a viable business proposition to large banks. On the other hand, however, it should not be overlooked that the peer pressure on lenders as well as their motivation is extremely high and that the default rates are negligible, which makes it an attractive proposition even in spite of the small ticket sizes.

14.3 The Case for LIBOR

The use of the London Interbank Offer Rate as a benchmark for the pricing of Islamic financial transactions is often received with scepticism, but still widely used in the absence of an alternative Islamic benchmark. A few alternatives have been reviewed, but till date, none holds up like LIBOR as a determinant of cost of funds, even though banks are at the moment of writing this book paying over the LIBOR rate due to the absence of available liquidity in the market. Desirable or not, there are a few strong reasons why LIBOR is till date still the benchmark of choice:

- **Availability of alternatives.** So far no viable alternative to LIBOR has been found that provides the same economic result of representing the cost of capital or cost of funds.

- **Incorporation of economic circumstances.** LIBOR as a measure of cost of funds incorporates the current economic climate as well as the growth expectation of the economy.

In addition, the majority of scholars are of the view that as long as the transaction fulfils all the requirements of *sharia'a*, using LIBOR as a benchmark to determine the profit of the underlying transaction is permissible. It does not render the transaction invalid since the transaction itself does not contain an interest element. In favour or against, for now it remains the most viable benchmark to determine the cost of funds.

15 Tax in the United Kingdom

Taxation rules are always a contentious subject, with governments trying to collect as much as possible and the public trying to pay as little as possible. It is no mere coincidence that SPVs and other structuring vehicles are always established in tax efficient jurisdictions.

Tax laws are typically written to cater for existing situations, and not with any implications of Islamic finance in mind. Due to the fact that the bank or other investors such as *sukuk* holders have some form of ownership over the assets they finance, issues such as double stamp duty land tax, capital gains tax and value added tax need to be considered carefully when structuring a transaction. In some jurisdictions it is not, or at least not yet, possible to avoid any disadvantageous tax related issues using any other structure than the *tawarruq* transaction. The United Kingdom, as part of its efforts to establish itself as the pre eminent centre of Islamic finance outside the Middle East and Asia, has started to make amendments to its taxation regime to allow alternative financial instruments to be treated at par with conventional instruments when it comes to taxation.

The combined changes made in the Finance Acts of 2005 and 2007 amount to the following:
- *Murabaha, musharaka, wakala* and *mudaraba* transactions are addressed in the Finance Act 2005.
- For taxation purposes, the revenue streams on *mudaraba, musharaka, wakala* and *mudaraba* transactions are treated similarly to interest income on conventional financing structures.
- The Finance Act 2007 addresses taxation issues associated with *sukuk* based on any of the above mentioned structures.
- No special provisions are made for *ijara*, since this structure is treated in the same was as a conventional sale and lease back.
- These changes are however mainly related to retail financing transactions, and do not necessarily cater for wholesale or corporate finance activities. Further changes are expected in the Finance Act 2009 and potentially beyond.

The impact of taxation is not the same in every country. In the Netherlands for instance, stamp duty land tax does not have to be paid on the sale of a property that is purchased and sold within six months time.

Unless changes are made in local tax regimes, however, Islamic financial structures will always raise a tax liability as a result of the fact the instruments have an underlying asset. Until such a change is made, *tawarruq* may in some countries be the only available instrument that does not disadvantage Islamic financial institutions in comparison to their conventional counterparts.

These are not the only issues that need to be taken into consideration however and any structure will need to be reviewed by a taxation expert in the relevant jurisdictions.

The remainder of this section provides more in-depth detail on VAT and Stamp Duty Land Tax for Islamic financial transactions in the United Kingdom. This section is contributed by the publisher with input from Ann Humphrey who specialises in taxation issues.

15.1 Tax Issues for Islamic Banking in the United Kingdom

Contributed by the publishers with assistance from Ann Humphrey (solicitor and tax advisor)

The UK Government's approach to the area of tax and Islamic finance was clearly set out in a document published at the time of the March 2005 Budget which stated:

> "The objective is to ensure that Sharia'a-compliant financial products are taxed in a way that is neither more nor less advantageous than equivalent banking products. The intended effect of the proposals is to allow providers to offer Sharia'a-compliant products without facing commercial disadvantage, and to enable customers to take up these products without encountering uncertainty or disadvantage over tax treatment."

Further insight into the direction of UK treatment of Islamic finance can be found in the consultation document on commercial *sukuk* published in June 2008. Much of this chapter is based on the information provided in that paper[26].

The UK tax problems are largely confined to the areas of VAT and stamp duty land tax (SDLT).

In this chapter we use the term "funder" to refer to all the different forms Islamic financial institutions can take (Bank, investment manager etc).

---

[26] The document can be downloaded from:

http://customs.hmrc.gov.uk/channelsPortalWebApp/channelsPortalWebApp.portal?_
nfpb=true&_pageLabel=pageLibrary_ConsultationDocuments&id=HMCE_PROD1_0286
85&propertyType=document

15.1.1 VAT and Islamic finance[27]

When considering the application of VAT to Islamic financial transactions, it is important to analyse all aspects of the service or product and consider the VAT treatment under the current rules.

The real challenge arises from the need to structure more complex Islamic financial services and products to be both *sharia'a* compliant and VAT efficient. For Islamic products and services such as savings accounts, loans, hire purchase transactions, insurance, bonds, etc, there is an element of buying and selling goods (for example, commodities) that needs to be taken into account. Where sale and purchase elements exist, there can be VAT complications. Furthermore, because VAT is a European Union tax, the process of changing VAT law can be more complex than changing other UK tax law, because of the need to keep the VAT treatment within the European legal framework.

15.1.1.1 Partnership contracts

The *mudarib* fee (or manager's fee), which relates specifically to the Islamic finance provider's profit, is charged for managing pooled assets. This could be regarded as the equivalent of a fund manager's fee and is therefore subject to VAT. However, it is part of the process of determining the profit element to be shared by the institution and the customers. This puts it outside the scope of UK VAT, as it would not be consideration for a supply. So, it is important to structure the fee as a share of or deduction from the overall profit in any terms and conditions in order to prevent a VAT charge arising.

15.1.1.2 Home Purchase Plans

As described in section 6.5, a *sharia'a*-compliant mortgage can be structured in using diminishing *musharaka*, lease, *murabaha* or a combination of diminishing *musharaka* and lease. In the UK, the FSA has regulated two different types of home purchase plans[28]:

Ijara **Home Purchase Plan**

A lender (the 'funder') purchases the property, either from the customer or from a seller identified by the funder's customer. The customer lives in the property and makes payments to the funder to repay them the exact purchase price, spread over a period. The customer is also charged rent for the proportion of the property he doesn't own. Once the purchase price has been

---

[27] This is discussed in more detail in an article *An Introduction to Islamic Banking* which appeared in *Tax Journal*, Issue 808, 10 October 2005.
[28] For more information on home purchase plans in the UK:
http://www.moneymadeclear.fsa.gov.uk/pdfs/home_purchase_plans.pdf

repaid the property is sold (or re-sold) to the customer. With the *ijara*, the monthly payments made towards buying the property are held by the firm and are used to buy the home at the end of the agreement.

This method is sometimes used for a joint purchase by the funder and the customer in which case the ownership is split in the ratio of funding contributed by the parties and the funder 'rents' its part of the property to the customer. Using this method the funder makes its profit from the rental payments for use of the proportion of the property he owns, rather than a charge for borrowing money.

Diminishing *Musharaka* Home Purchase Plan

A funder purchases the property (either from the customer or from a seller identified by the funder's customer) and sells it on to the customer at an agreed higher price to be paid over a period. The funder's profit arises from the profit on the sale of the property. With each payment the client makes towards buying the property he buys an additional slice of the funder's share. As the share of the funder decreases, the buyer's share increases and he pays a smaller amount of rent.

Both the above mentioned methods of lending against the property are structured so that the same property is bought and sold twice (that is, the seller who may be the customer or a third party sells to the funder which then, in turn, sells (or sells back) to the customer). This ensures that the funder can charge a 'profit element' rather than interest. At present, the bulk of *sharia'a* compliant mortgages are residential and VAT exemptions will apply. However, for non-residential mortgages, the situation could be quite complex in view of the application of the option to tax and the range of other rules which could apply. The key objective would be to ensure that there is no unanticipated VAT cost in any proposed transaction. The SDLT consequences of these transactions are dealt with in section 15.2 below.

15.1.1.3 Cost plus financing

The final Islamic financial product to consider in relation to VAT is the 'white-goods' *murabaha*, which is designed as a financing facility to enable customers to buy consumer goods. As described in section 6.6.1, the structure works as follows:

* the customer identifies the goods they are interested in purchasing;
* the customer and the funder agree a profit margin and the institution purchases the goods from the vendor;
* the customer takes possession of the physical goods acting as agent of the institution, while the bank obtains the title to the goods;

- the institution then sells the goods to the customer based on cost plus the agreed profit margin which is payable over an agreed period; and
- the title to the goods passes to the customer at the time the sale occurs.

The *murabaha* competes with the conventional hire purchase and credit sale arrangements. The sale of the conventional products would be treated as VATable with the credit charge being treated as VAT exempt. On the face of it, the profit element of a sale of VATable goods in a *murabaha* transaction would not be exempt. So, it is important to ensure that the contracts relating to the arrangements reflect the requirements for conventional VAT exempt credit sale agreements such as the disclosure of the profit element and the fact that there is a higher charge for the longer deferment terms.

Example – potential VAT implication of consumer financing using *murabaha*

A client wishes to purchase a new fridge using Islamic finance, which leads to the following steps being taken:

1. Client identifies the fridge for which the price is £500 including 17.5% VAT (£425.53 + £74.47 VAT);
2. Bank purchase the fridge for £500 and sells it on to the client at a deferred payment for the purchase price plus a mark-up of £50 to be paid in 3 months time;

Due to the fact that a sale is involved, the bank technically has to charge the client £425.53 plus the mark-up of £50 and has to charge 17.5% VAT over the total amount thus resulting in a total sale price to the client of £475.53 * 1.175 = £558.78

However, by categorising the transaction as a conventional credit sale for VAT purposes, the customer only pays £550.

One of the complications of VAT is that a supply may fall into one of four categories:

- Standard-rated (currently 17.5% in the UK and varies across Europe)
- Reduced-rate (currently 5% in the UK, and the list of reduced-rate supplies is set out in Schedule 7A of VATA 1994)
- Zero-rated (set out in Schedule 8, VATA 1994), and
- Exempt supplies (set out in Schedule 9 VATA 1994).

The category of exempt supplies was agreed when VAT was introduced across the EEC. Zero-rated and reduced-rate supplies have been negotiated on a national basis.

15.1.2   VAT compliance

This section looks into issues such as how the additional transactions necessary to achieve a *sharia'a* compliant facility will be treated within a special partial exemption method, how the buying and selling of taxable goods affect a loan facility and the effect of the high values from one-off commodity transactions that Islamic finance providers which often match.

15.1.2.1 Commodities

Commodities play an important role in Islamic financial transactions due to the fact that the transaction needs to have an underlying asset. The rules for commodities are very complex and require careful management. Some of the issues to consider are:

- If dealing in metal, is the metal allocated or unallocated? The former is viewed as a supply of goods, with the latter being viewed as a supply of services for the purposes of determining the place of supply and the VAT liability of such transactions.
- Is the place of supply in the UK? Europe? Outside Europe? In a bonded warehouse? All of these factors will affect the VAT liability.

If the transaction benefits from relief under the Terminal Markets Order, the supply will be zero-rated (see HMRC Notice 701/9 (March 2002)).

The commodity itself may be zero-rated (Schedule 8, VATA 1994).

15.1.2.2 Interest

To be *sharia'a* compliant a funder would not want to apply default interest charges, so other charges need to be applied. Conversely it would not want to be paid statutory interest (or would want to ensure that it is donated to charity).

15.1.3   The VAT issue going forward

HM Revenue and Customs and HM Treasury appreciate the challenges that Islamic finance creates in the area of VAT. HM Treasury has established the HM Treasury Islamic Experts Group and HM Revenue and Customs (HMRC) have created the HMRC Islamic Finance Group.

15.2 Stamp Duty Land Tax[29]

The structure used for *sharia'a* compliant mortgages would typically result in SDLT being borne twice - once by the funder and again by the customer when ownership transfers to the ultimate buyer – whereas a conventional mortgage funding would involve only one charge to SDLT. Consequently, *sharia'a* compliant mortgages would have resulted in an additional SDLT cost.

Relief from multiple charges to SDLT is available for several types of alternative finance schemes. These reliefs were, until 19 July 2006, relevant to individuals only but were extended to persons other than individuals (i.e. to companies, trusts, charities and partnerships) by section 168 FA 2006. No alternative property finance relief is available where the 'first transaction' is one to which any of the reliefs under Schedule 7 FA 2003 (group, reconstruction and acquisition reliefs) apply. This ensures that only one relief is claimed, and is an anti-avoidance provision consequent on the extension of the alternative property finance reliefs to companies. The reliefs are set out in sections 71A to 73 of FA 2003.

As mentioned in the introduction to this chapter, HMRC issued a consultation document entitled *Stamp duty land tax: Commercial sukuk* on 27 June 2008, concerning the Government's attempts to offset any SDLT consequences arising on the issuance of a commercial *sukuk*. The document helpfully set out what measures the Government has taken to date and what further action is intended to enable *sharia'a*-compliant financial products to compete with the traditional finance sector without being at a tax disadvantage. Set out below are relevant extracts from the consultation document which provide information on the current and proposed tax position. The consultation closed on 18 August 2008, and no draft legislation for FA 2009 was available before this publication went to press.

15.3 Background to the UK Government Policies

As part of the Government's policy on City competitiveness to facilitate innovation in the financial services sector, Islamic finance has been identified as an important, high-growth area. The Government's objective for Islamic finance is two-fold:
1. to establish London as a global gateway for Islamic finance; and
2. to ensure that all British citizens, regardless of their faith, have access to competitive financial services.

---

[29] For a full account of these reliefs see Stamp Duty Land Tax (second edition) by Ann Humphrey and Philip Freedman (Spiramus Press, 2007).

Since 2003, the Government has worked steadily towards its aim to ensure a 'level playing field' for both retail and wholesale Islamic financial products against existing financial products. The Government is continuing to deliver changes to facilitate growth in this area.

In the Budget 2007, the Government announced a package of measures reflecting market developments over the past 12 months, including a new special tax regime for listed *sukuk* (see section **Error! Reference source not found.** above). *Sukuk* are Islamic financial certificates, equivalent to bonds that comply with the requirements of *sharia'a*. The Government measures enable *sukuk* to be held, issued and traded in the same way as corporate bonds.

15.3.1 Changes to Taxation and Regulatory Policy since 2003

Over the past few years, a number of changes have been introduced to the taxation and regulatory policy in the UK to accommodate alternative financial products in general. Although introduced to facilitate Islamic financial structures, they are not limited to these. The remainder of this section outlines the changes to the Finance Act in the various years since 2003. No changes were introduced in the Finance Act 2004.

15.3.1.1 Changes in 2003

The first tax legislation catering specifically for Islamic financial arrangements came in Finance Act 2003, in the area of SDLT. This removed a major obstacle to the marketing of *sharia'a* compliant mortgages by introducing reliefs to prevent multiple payments of SDLT for these transactions (see above).

The FSA consulted on whether to regulate Islamic home financing, in order to give consumers broadly the same protection as consumers of conventional mortgages. This resulted in the authorisation of the *murabaha* method in October 2004 and *ijara* (lease to own) home purchase plans after FA 2007.

15.3.1.2 Changes in 2005

In 2005 Government created a 'level playing field' for tax purposes for *mudaraba* and *murabaha* products that are equivalent to deposits and loan financing. The Government also introduced further changes to SDLT legislation to extend relief from multiple SDLT to a newly available shared ownership product known as diminishing *musharaka* and to ensure that the existing *ijara wa iqtina* (lease ending in ownership) relief for home purchase plans was effective throughout the UK.

15.3.1.3 Changes in 2006

The changes in the 2006 Finance Act can be summarised as follows:

- HMRC enabled the use of diminishing *musharaka* (reducing partnership)

products in place of standard loans.
- As part of leasing reform, legislation was introduced enabling the use of *ijara wa iqtina* for asset finance.
- SDLT reliefs for Islamic products were extended to companies.
- Secondary legislation bringing Home Purchase Plans (HPPs) into regulation by the Financial Services Authority (FSA) was enacted.

15.3.1.4 Changes in 2007
In the Finance Act 2007, the following changes were introduced:

- Introduction of legislation to clarify the taxation of *sukuk*. Regulations were introduced detailing stock exchanges recognised for the purposes of *sukuk*.
- Regulations introduced to extend the Community Investment Tax Relief scheme to include Islamic financial products.
- Guidance on treatment of diminishing *musharaka* for capital gains and capital allowance and clarification of tax treatment of *Takaful* (Islamic insurance), Real Estate Investment Trusts (REITs) and Private Finance Initiative (PFI).
- The FSA commenced regulation of *ijara* (lease to own) home purchase plans.
- HM Treasury and Debt Management Office (DMO) announced a study into the feasibility of Government sukuk issuance.
- National Savings & Investment announced decision to look at the feasibility of Government issuing retail Islamic products as part of implementation of new 5-year strategy.

In the same year, the FSA published a paper with the title *"Islamic Finance in the UK: Regulation and Challenges"*[30], which sets out the regulatory steps taken to ensure that London can compete internationally as a hub for Islamic finance.

15.3.2 Announcements in 2008

At the Budget 2008, the Government announced its intention to:

- Introduce legislation in Finance Bill 2009 to provide relief from SDLT for alternative finance investment bonds, following a formal consultation, making it possible for UK based corporations to issue *sukuk* as an alternative means of funding.
- Amend legislation to classify alternative finance investment bonds as loan capital for the purposes of stamp duty and stamp duty reserve tax (SDRT).

---

[30] http://www.fsa.gov.uk/pubs/other/islamic_finance.pdf

- Introduce legislation to allow existing corporation tax and income tax rules on alternative finance arrangements to be amended by regulation if and when required.

The FSA announced its attention to clarify the regulatory treatment of *sukuk*, consulting with stakeholders where appropriate (see 15.3.2.1 below).

15.3.2.1 Commercial Sukuk: current SDLT treatment

Sukuk, which are described in detail in section 4.4.2, are economically similar to Eurobonds and structured in a way similar to a securitisation transaction, a form of corporate finance in which assets are transferred to a special purpose vehicle (SPV), which then issues bonds to third party investors in capital markets, secured on those assets. The individual investment certificate (*sakk*) evidences a proportional share in the beneficial ownership of an underlying asset.

Sukuk may often be backed by land or property as the underlying asset, or any other tangible asset. In a normal securitisation transaction the investor does not have a direct ownership share in the underlying asset but merely an interest-bearing certificate, whereas in a *sukuk* the investors own a proportional part of the underlying asset.

SDLT is a charge on the acquisition of a chargeable interest in UK land whether or not evidenced in writing. This is a departure from stamp duty, which is a tax on the stamped document which formally records a transaction and still applies to the sale and purchase of shares. SDLT was introduced to eliminate the practice of "resting on contract" whereby a property transaction was deliberately left uncompleted to avoid paying stamp duty. Issuing a conventional bond secured on a building does not cause any SDLT to arise.

However, in a *sukuk* structure, in order to be *sharia'a* compliant the originator must sell an asset to a SPV, which is subsequently divided into equal units and sold to the investors. SDLT will therefore be charged if a chargeable asset such as a building is transferred to an SPV that issues a sukuk, and is charged again when the originator buys back the building. (SDLT is generally not chargeable on the rent payable by the originator to the SPV, as "sale and leaseback relief" should be available).

It has been Government policy to date to ensure that where practical, *sharia'a* compliant financial products should be taxed on an equivalent basis with conventional products. At present a SDLT charge on *sukuk* places an additional barrier to issuance compared with a conventional equivalent and inhibits the UK Government's two-fold aims on Islamic finance: first to boost London's position as an international financial hub (the UK government's aim is for London to be the largest Islamic Financial centre outside the Middle East and

Asia); and, secondly to encourage greater social and financial inclusion among its two million Muslims.

Working under a standard *sukuk al ijara* and in applying current legislation to any *sukuk* issuance, there is the potential for the *sukuk* to be subject to SDLT charges if the property is UK land or property qualifying as a chargeable asset

As described in section 4.4.2.4, a *sukuk al ijara* is typically a sale and lease back structure and can graphically be depicted as follows:

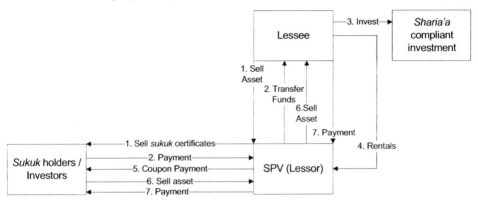

Figure 47: *Sukuk al ijara*

SDLT can occur at the following points in the transaction:

1. **SDLT charge 1 – Step 1, Sell Asset**
    SPV purchasing asset from originator. SDLT will be payable by the purchaser (the SPV) on the acquisition of a chargeable interest in land at a rate of four per cent (assuming that the asset is valued at more than £500,000).

2. **SDLT charge 2 – Step 6, Sell Asset**
    Originator, purchasing asset from SPV. On the winding up of the sukuk, the originator will purchase the asset back from the SPV. SDLT will be payable by the purchaser (this time the originator) on the acquisition of a chargeable interest in land at a rate of four per cent (assuming again that the asset is valued at more than £500,000).

3. **SDLT charge 3 - Step 1, Sell *sukuk* certificates**
    There is also some uncertainty as to whether sukuk certificate buyers would be liable to SDLT as the certificate will evidence their interest in an underlying chargeable asset.

These extra SDLT charges put a sukuk structure at a considerable disadvantage compared to their conventional equivalent.

It is therefore considered desirable that SDLT should not be charged when land is sold to the issuer of a *sukuk*, and that no SDLT is charged on the sale back of the building to the originator. The sale of *sukuk* bonds should also not attract any SDLT.

15.3.2.2 Proposed Legislative Framework

Set out below is a summary of proposed SDLT relief on alternative finance investment bond transactions

A. The relief will be self-certified.

B. In order to obtain the relief the sukuk must fall within requirements of s48A of FA 2005 (alternative finance investment bonds).

C. The following transactions will be exempt:
    i) The transfer from originator to the SPV.
    ii) The transfer back from the SPV to the originator.
    iii) The issue and resale of sukuk bonds.

D. Legislation to be introduced in Finance Bill 2009 to provide specific relief.

Relief available on transfer to the Special Purpose Vehicle

The transfer of the property from the originator to the SPV will be exempt providing that the following conditions are satisfied:

*   The asset must be defined and returned to the originator within the same period as the bond issuance.

*   The *sukuk* issuer would need to identify a UK agent who would become liable for SDLT should the asset not return to the originator.

Relief available on transfer to back to originator

The transfer of the asset back to the originator will be exempt.

If the defined asset is not returned to the originator then an SDLT charge will arise on the SPV or any company within the SPV group. This requirement would be extended to the new group if the SPV is sold.

If it is not possible to recover SDLT from the SPV or any company within the SPV group, then the UK agent will become liable for any SDLT.

Relief on sukuk issuance and sale on secondary market

The initial issue and subsequent resale on secondary markets of the bonds would be exempt.

The *sukuk* issuer must issue bonds up to the value of at least 95 per cent of asset.

To address avoidance risks the Government would like to encourage wide ownership of bonds. For example, if one person acquired 10 per cent or more of the total *sukuk* then any income generated above that level would be restricted.

Statutory conditions for alternative finance investment bonds

Sukuk arrangements are capable of taking a wide variety of forms. Those which fall within the alternative finance legislation are those which function economically as debt securities.

FA 2005 section 48A(1) lays down a number of conditions that alternative finance investment bonds must satisfy, and FA 2005 section 48A(2) provides a further gloss on the conditions. These conditions are set out below:

- The arrangements provide for one person, described in the legislation as the bond- holder, to pay a sum of money ("the capital") to another person, described as the bond-issuer.

- The arrangements must identify assets, or a class of assets ("the **bond assets**"). In many cases, this "identification" will take the form of the issuer making a Declaration of Trust in respect of the assets. Particularly where the arrangements are not governed by English law, however, the sukuk holders' interest in the assets may take some different legal form: this does not prevent the arrangements from coming within section 48A.

- The bond-issuer must acquire the bond assets in order to generate income or gains. The requirement for the issuer to acquire assets means that arrangements under which an issuing company pledges existing assets as collateral for borrowing, or where a charge is created over particular assets of the issuer, do not come within the legislation.

- The arrangements must have a fixed term or maturity date. This distinguishes alternative finance investment bonds from, for example, collective investment schemes, where the investor's interest in the scheme may subsist indefinitely. But arrangements are not disqualified because investors (usually by majority vote in a general meeting) may have the right to require the trust to be dissolved early in certain circumstances.

- Under the arrangements, the bond-holders must be entitled to two sorts of payment. At the end of the bond term, the bond-issuer must dispose of the remaining bond assets, and make a payment to the bond-holder - described as the **redemption payment** - to repay the capital subscribed. The bond-holder must also receive **additional payments**, either during the term of the bond or at maturity, or both.

- The amount of the additional payments must not exceed a **reasonable commercial return**.

- The arrangements must allow the bond issuer to **manage the assets** so as to generate sufficient income to make the redemption payments and the additional payment.

- The alternative finance bonds must be **listed on a recognised stock exchange**. They must also be transferable - although listed securities will always fulfil this condition.

- The arrangements must be wholly or partly treated in accordance with international accounting standards as a **financial liability**.

15.3.2.3   Tax treatment of alternative finance investment bonds

Where *sukuk* meet the conditions in FA 2005 section48A to be alternative finance investment bonds additional payments made or received under the bonds are alternative finance return. This is subject to the provisions about discount.

For corporation tax purposes, FA 2005 section 50 treats alternative finance investment bonds as loan relationships.

For income tax purposes, FA 2005 section 51 applies to alternative finance return received or paid on such bonds. There are further statutory provisions for alternative finance investment bonds, which are relevant only to non-corporate holders.

Where an alternative finance investment bond is treated as a loan relationship, FA 1996 section 80(5) ensures that profits or losses from the bond cannot be taxed or relieved in any other way. But because many, if not most, *sukuk* arrangements:

- involve the creation of a trust; and

- fall to be treated as collective investment schemes under Financial Services and Markets Act 2000.

The legislation provides that tax provisions relevant to trusts or to collective investment schemes do not apply.

Specifically, FA 2005 section 48B(5) ensures that alternative finance investment bonds are not treated as a unit trust scheme either for the purposes of ICTA 1988 section 469 or ITA 2007 section 1007 (dealing with the taxation of unauthorised unit trusts) or for capital gains purposes; not treated as an offshore fund; and, for a company, are not a "relevant holding" in a unit trust or offshore fund for loan relationships purposes.

16 Capital Adequacy under Basel II

16.1 Introduction

Since the Islamic financial industry is young and the balance sheet size of the average Islamic bank is relatively small, issues associated with the calculation of regulatory capital are in part similar to those faced by small, locally operating, conventional European and North American banks. However, because of the transaction structures employed, Islamic banks may face higher charges for regulatory capital under the Basel II capital accord[31].

There are, in fact, a few Islamic Finance specific issues that need to be taken into consideration when contemplating the potential impact of the Basel II implementation at Islamic banks. This chapter first outlines the capital adequacy and minimum capital requirements and then explores the different risk types Islamic banks are exposed to in comparison to conventional banks. This is followed by an outline of the new capital adequacy requirements defined by the IFSB for Islamic banks. Finally the capital adequacy requirements for *sukuk* in three different global jurisdictions - Malaysia, Bahrain and the United Kingdom, are explored in further detail.

16.2 Capital Adequacy and Minimum Capital Requirements

Capital adequacy is a measure of the ability of a bank or securities firm to absorb unexpected losses, typically expressed as a ratio of capital to risk weighted assets. Banks typically require a larger amount of capital to cover unexpected losses than securities firms since the latter can unwind positions quicker and are affected less by a reduction of available liquidity in the markets. The Basel II capital accord provides financial services regulators with a framework that allows them to manage the capital adequacy of the banks under their supervision. The Basel II accord – originally intended for large internationally active banks in the G10 countries – is being implemented by a large number of countries outside the G10, and is in most cases applied to all banks in the regulator's jurisdiction regardless of whether they are internationally active.

---

[31] Basel Committee of Banking Supervision (2006) *Basel II: International Convergence of Capital Measurement and Capital Standards: A Revised Framework* June 2006

CAPITAL ADEQUACY UNDER BASEL II

Under the capital adequacy regime, banks are required to hold a minimum level of capital to prevent over lending and to ensure that every bank has sufficient funds in case any of its counterparties default without endangering depositors, the banking system or the economy as a whole. The minimum level of capital required equals the total of risk weighted assets multiplied by the Capital Adequacy Requirement (CAR), which is generally set at 8% but is subject to supervisory discretion and could potentially be higher (e.g. in Bahrain it is set at 12%).

The constituents of capital have not changed between Basel I and Basel II, and are defined as follows[32]:

1. Core Capital (basic equity or Tier 1 capital). Core capital consists of equity capital and disclosed reserves. Equity capital includes issued and fully paid up ordinary shares and non-cumulative perpetual preferred stock but excludes cumulative preferred stock. Core capital should comprise at least 50% of the bank's total capital base.
2. Supplementary Capital (Tier 2) consists of other capital elements which may be considered by the regulator.
   a. Undisclosed or hidden reserves which are unpublished but have passed through the profit and loss account and are accepted by the regulatory authorities;
   b. Revaluation reserves arising from formal revaluations or from a notional addition to capital. Revaluation reserves may be included provided that the regulator considers the assets to be prudently valued, fully reflecting the possibility of price fluctuation and forced sale. Revaluation reserves have to be subject to a 55% discount to reflect concerns about market volatility and tax charges in the event of realised profits;
   c. General provisions and general loan loss reserves created against unidentified future losses as long as they do not reflect a known deterioration in the value of particular assets. General provisions included in Tier 2 capital are subject to a limit which is expressed as a % of risk weighted assets and depends on the approach the bank is taking to credit risk;

---

[32] Basel Committee of Banking Supervision (2006) *Basel II: International Convergence of Capital Measurement and Capital Standards: A Revised Framework*, paragraph 49

    d. Hybrid debt capital instruments cover instruments that have both equity and debt characteristics. Hybrid debt capital instruments can be included when they have close similarities to equity, in particular when they are able to support losses on an on-going basis without triggering liquidation.

    e. Subordinated term debt with a minimum original term to maturity of five years or longer can be included limited to a maximum of 50% of core capital.

3. Short-term subordinated debt covering market risk (Tier 3) consists of other capital elements which may be considered by the regulator but is subject to strict criteria and limits.

4. Deductions from capital which consist of goodwill, increase in equity capital resulting from a securitisation exposure and investments in subsidiaries in banking and financial activities not consolidated in national systems.

In addition, Basel II maintains the minimum requirement of 8% of capital to risk weighted assets. Although there are no changes to the calculation of capital for market risk beyond the specification of the 1996 Market Risk Amendment to Basel I, market risk is now specifically segregated from credit risk (it was previously taken into consideration in the overall RWA calculation). Moreover, Basel II has introduced a capital charge for operational risk and it has placed greater emphasis on credit risk measurement and mitigation techniques.

The original capital adequacy rules came into effect in 1988, are generally known as Basel I, and are still in use in a large number of countries outside the G10. Within this framework, only credit risk and market risk have an impact on the level of regulatory capital. Each asset on the bank's balance sheet is assigned a risk weight as illustrated in the table below.

Example Asset Classes	Risk Weight
Central governments, central banks, OECD governments	0%
Multilateral development banks, banks incorporated in the OECD	20%
Mortgages	50%
Private sector, commercial companies owned by the public sector, all other assets	100%

Table 11: Basel I Asset Classes

Risk Weighted Assets (RWA) are determined by multiplying the outstanding exposures per counterparty by the risk weight that applies to the type of counterparty. Risk mitigation such as netting and pledged deposits can be applied to reduce RWA as long as a set of predefined conditions are met. Regulatory capital is then determined as the aggregate of all RWAs multiplied by 8 percent. The 8% ratio is set by the Basel Committee of Banking Supervision (BCBS) on the basis that it would result in sufficient levels of capital held in the banking sector to cover potential defaults.

Basel I was the first, fairly basic, framework to measuring capital adequacy and one of the main issues with the implementation lies in the fact that there is no distinction between high- and low-quality borrowers. This becomes immediately apparent from the examples in the box below.

Box 1 - No distinction in borrower quality

> National Grid Group, one of the world's largest utilities companies, and Enron are both classified as "corporates." Their exposures are risk weighted at 100 percent and this applied even when it started to became evident that Enron had a much lower credit quality. For every £100 of credit extended to each of these borrowers, the bank has to maintain £100 * 100% * 8% = £8 in capital.
>
> The National Bank for Foreign Economic Activity of the Republic of Uzbekistan and HSBC are both classified as "banks," which means their exposures attract a 20 percent risk weight. This implies that for every £100 of credit extended to them, the bank only has to maintain £100 * 20% * 8% = £1.60 in capital.
>
> In both cases, the chances of either party defaulting differ significantly due to their credit quality. However, the amount of capital required on their exposure remains the same.

There are more disadvantages to Basel I, such as the fact that there is no distinction between long and short-term loans and the limited use of risk-mitigating techniques, which the BCBS attempted to address in the Basel II framework.

The intention of Basel II is to address the shortcomings that are inherent in the Basel I accord. It introduces counterparty grading to overcome the fact that there is currently no distinction between low and high-quality borrowers. In addition, it introduces operational risk and market discipline. Basel II is organised around three mutually reinforcing pillars: minimum capital requirement, supervisory review and market discipline.

Pillar 1: Minimum Capital Requirements

The new framework maintains both the current definition of capital and the minimum requirement of 8 percent of capital to RWA. There is an increased emphasis on credit risk measurement and mitigation techniques. Market risk, which was previously taken into consideration in the overall RWA calculation, is now segregated from credit risk. A capital charge is introduced for operational risk. The Basel II framework does not introduce any changes to the calculation of capital for market risk beyond the specification of the 1996 market risk amendment to Basel I.

For both the credit and operational risk components, three different approaches are available, each with a different level of sophistication.

Box 2 - Basel II approaches for credit risk

> Credit risk is defined as the risk that a counterparty will default on one or more of his payments. Three approaches can be used to determine the required capital:
>
> *Standardised Approach*
>
> The standardised approach is roughly the same as the current Basel I approach. In addition to the standard risk weights currently available, clients need to be graded by an External Credit Assessment Institution (ECAI). The rating of the counterparty is now incorporated into the overall risk weighting. In the absence of an external rating, the counterparty attracts a risk weight of 100%.
>
> *Foundation Internal Ratings Based Approach (FIRB)*
>
> Banks do not rely on ECAIs for their ratings, but determine the probability of default (PD) of their borrowers using an internally built model. Loss given default (LGD) and exposure at default (EAD) are determined based on supervisory rules defined in the Accord.
>
> *Advanced Internal Ratings Based (AIRB)*
>
> Not only the PD, but also LGD and EAD are determined based on internally built models.

Box 3 - Basel II approaches for operational risk

Operational risk is defined as the risk of loss resulting from inadequate or failed internal processes, people and systems or from external events. This includes legal risk, but excludes strategic and reputational risk. Similar to the calculation of the minimum capital requirements for credit risk, three methodologies are available for the calculation of operational risk capital charges:

Basic Indicator Approach

Capital charge is calculated as a fixed percentage (15%) of average gross income over the previous three years. The percentage is determined by the regulator.

Standardised Approach

The banks' activities are divided into eight business lines and the capital charge is calculated per business line as a percentage of gross income. The percentages differ according to the business line and are set by the regulators

Advanced Measurement Approach (AMA)

Under the AMA approach, banks apply their own internally developed model which incorporates quantitative and qualitative criteria such as internal loss data, key risk indicators, scenario analysis and self-assessment.

Generally, it is expected that large banks with sophisticated risk management systems will benefit from the new regulation and see their capital reduced as a result of applying the more advanced approaches. However, this also strongly depends on overall counterparty credit quality and robustness of internal control processes and procedures. Smaller banks, however, may not be able to justify investments on the same scale, and will therefore not be in a position to benefit from the advanced risk measurement approaches.

Islamic banks certainly fall under the smaller banks category, but they also face some other issues that are uncommon to the rest of the financial industry.

Pillar 2: Supervisory Review

Supervisors are required to ensure that each bank under its supervision has sound internal processes in place to assess the adequacy of its capital. Typically they employ an internal capital adequacy assessment process (ICAAP) which is prepared by banks and reviewed by supervisors. In addition, specific review visits are part of this process. The supervisor can request additional regulatory capital for any issues not covered under Pillar I, such as interest rate risk in the banking book and concentration risk.

Pillar 3: Market Discipline

The majority of disclosures are recommended and not mandatory. The intention is to reduce potential overhead with other disclosure standards such as IFRS and IAS. As a result, additional disclosures are only mandatory in relation to the implementation of particular methodologies or instruments.

The general expectation is that large banks with sophisticated risk management systems will benefit from the new regulation and for the same assets will see their regulatory capital level reduced. However, this will strongly depend on overall counterparty credit quality and robustness of internal control processes and procedures. For the industry as a whole, the required capital is expected to remain as is, or potentially even increase.

16.3 Challenges in Islamic Finance

For conventional banks, part of regulatory capital is absorbed by interest rate risk in the banking book. The absence of interest in Islamic Finance means that Islamic banks are not subject to interest rate risk, but instead face rate of return risk which is in some ways analogous to 'interest rate risk in the banking book'. Islamic banks are not subject to lower levels of risk and subsequently regulatory capital than conventional banks.

As outlined earlier, like conventional banks, Islamic banks incur liquidity, credit, settlement, leverage, operational and business risk. Liquidity risk for Islamic banks is more difficult to manage and more expensive than for conventional banks due to the absence of liquid and accepted primary liquidity instruments (i.e. Certificates of Deposit (CDs), Commercial Paper (CPs) and Treasury Bills (T-Bills). Government Securities such as T-Bonds and Gilts as well as Eurobonds and domestic bonds are not permissible, and although few instruments such as the Bahraini government 90-day *sukuk al salam,* which is a type of non-negotiable T-Bill, are available, they are still limited. In addition, as noted in chapter 12, Islamic banks also incur risks that are not common in conventional banks, such as fiduciary risk, displaced commercial risk and rate of return risk.

This section looks into some of the challenges the Islamic banking industry sector faces with the implementation of the Basel II framework. Similar to Basel II for conventional banks, a number of implementation rules are subject to supervisory discretion, leading to differences in the requirements in different countries[33].

16.3.1 Balance Sheet Size and Loss Data History

Although the Islamic financial industry has grown substantially over the past decade, it remains small when compared to the overall financial sector. Indeed, the size of an individual Islamic bank is typically not large enough to justify the investment required for the advanced risk measurement approaches. As mentioned earlier, this is not a problem that is exclusive to Islamic banks, but the relative small size of the Islamic financial industry makes it more difficult to lobby for changes in global regulatory policy, such as Basel II.

The absence of significant amounts of loss data is one of the problems that hinder smaller sized banks that need to comply with Basel II. Islamic banks – most of which have only recently been established and which have not seen a complete economic cycle yet – do not have a long enough history and hence can not meet the Basel II requirement for seven years of loss data. Although this is also a problem all new smaller banks, conventional European and North American banks have the opportunity to join one of the established data consortia - such as the Pan European Credit Data Consortium (PECDC) or the North American Loan Loss Database (NALLD) to gain access to a larger data set with a longer history of loss data. The IFSB is currently working on a similar database for Islamic banks, but it is not yet available.

16.3.2 Equity Treatment

With the introduction of Basel II, significant equity positions are treated separately from other (i.e. debt) financing. The underlying principle of the Basel Committee of Banking Supervision's (BCBS) stance on equity holding is that a bank is exposed to higher risk when ownership and the provision of debt funding are in the same hands. This causes a challenge for Islamic banks, because *mudaraba* and *musharaka* financing assets that are based on profit-

---

[33] It is worth noting that Islamic financial institutions have a lot in common with securities firms and in principle do not have to hold capital against balances in Investment Accounts due to the fact that losses associated with investment accounts are passed on to the investment account holders and are not a liability of the bank. Due to commercial and, in some cases, legal pressure however, this is not the case in all jurisdictions.

sharing principles may be deemed to be similar to holding equity positions in the banking book from a regulatory perspective.

As a result of the introduction of the new framework, banks that hold equity positions (e.g. *mudaraba* and *musharaka* assets) may be heavily penalised in terms of regulatory capital. Specifically, under the Basel II standards on capital adequacy, transactions that are based on profit sharing and loss bearing modes carry a very high risk weight of 400%. The Islamic Financial Services Board's (IFSB) guidelines for capital adequacy[34] translate the Basel II framework to the specific Islamic financial products, and incorporate the same view on equity type positions. Alternatively, however, the IFSB Standard includes risk weights based on the 'supervisory slotting' criteria in Basel II for specialised financing which can be applied to *mudaraba* and *musharaka* assets at the discretion of the supervisor. The treatment of the individual transaction types for capital adequacy is outlined in more detail in the next section.

16.4 IFSB Capital Adequacy Standards

The IFSB capital adequacy standards deals with all types of products an Islamic bank offers. Most current IFSB standards only apply to Islamic financial institutions solely offering Islamic financial services and explicitly exclude insurance institutions. However, separate standards for governance and capital adequacy for insurance companies are being developed and a standard for business conduct, which is currently being finalised, will apply to both financial services and insurance companies.

16.4.1 The Definition of Capital

The IFSB guidelines define capital as consisting of Tier 1 and Tier 2 capital, with Tier 1 capital constituting at least 50% of the total capital base. Tier 1 and 2 capital are made up of the following components:

1. Core Capital (basic equity or Tier 1 capital). Core capital consists of equity capital, disclosed reserves, retained profit, unrealised net gains from fair valuation of equity and minority interests in subsidiaries. Equity capital consists of issued and fully paid up ordinary shares. Core capital should comprise at least 50% of the bank's total capital base. The shareholders'

---

[34] Islamic Financial Services Board (2005) *Capital Adequacy Standard for Institutions (Other than Insurance Institutions) Offering Only Islamic Financial Services* December 2005

portion of the profit equalisation reserve is technically a category of retained profit, and would therefore classify as Tier 1 capital.[35]

2. Supplementary Capital (Tier 2) consists of other capital elements which may be considered by the regulator.
   a. Current interim retained profits;
   b. Revaluation reserves arising from the revaluation of fixed assets and real estate in line with changes in market values. Revaluation reserves have to be subject to a 55% discount to historic book value to reflect concerns about market volatility and tax charges in the event of realised profits;
   c. Unrealised gains arising from fair valuing equities, subject to a discount factor of 55%.

3. Deductions from capital which consist of goodwill, interim cumulative net losses, unrealised gross losses arising from fair valuation of equity securities and reciprocal cross holdings of other banks' capital.

Contrary to the BCBS, the IFSB only recognises Tier 1 and Tier 2 capital, with Tier 1 capital being at least 50% of the total capital base.

16.4.2 Credit Risk Mitigation

Any credit risk attached to a transaction and its counterparty can be mitigated by applying a number of techniques, which can be summarised as follows:

- **Security deposit**. A refundable security deposit taken by the bank as a deposit prior to concluding the contract and will cover any opportunity cost incurred in the event the client decides not to execute the contract. The security deposit only offers limited recourse, and any cost over and beyond the amount of the security deposit can not be recovered.
- **Deposit**. Financial deposits held for the duration of the contract accrue to the investor if the client breaches the contract part way through.
- **Third party guarantee.** Guarantees provided by a third party to cover any claims in the event of a default. Guarantees can be limited in time and amount.

---

[35] The Investment Account Holder portion of these reserves does not qualify as capital due to the fact that they are not attributable to shareholders. Under the Basel II capital rules the shareholder portion could be classified as Tier 1 capital as they are a classification of retained earnings. It could, however, be considered more prudent to treat this portion of the reserve as Tier 2 capital due to lack of transparency in appropriations to the reserve. The Investment Risk Reserve does not have a shareholder portion, and as such does not qualify as capital.

- **Assets pledged.** Assets pledged as collateral need to be *sharia'a* compliant, fully owned and saleable. Any assets pledged only qualify as collateral if the pledge is legally enforceable.
- **Leased assets.** Any leased assets are owned by the bank and can be used to mitigate any risk.

Generally, collateral will reduce the risk of the bank and consequently reduces the capital charge a transaction attracts, although for capital adequacy purposes not all collateral is eligible for capital relief. Any unsecured portion of the transaction attracts the risk weight of the counterparty. Capital relief can be granted according to the following two approaches:

- **Simple Approach.** In the simple approach, the bank substitutes the risk weight of the counterparty with the risk weight of the collateral, subject to a minimum risk weight of 20%. A 0% risk weight may be applied when the collateral is in cash on deposit in the same currency or the collateral is in the form of sovereign securities eligible for 0% risk weight and for which the market value is discounted by 20%.
- **Haircuts.** Both the original exposure and the collateral are adjusted by a haircut that is either defined by the supervisor or calculated internally.

16.4.3 Market Risk

Market risk, represents the risk that the bank's position – whether on or off balance sheet – becomes impaired. The IFSB capital adequacy guidelines recognise three forms of market risk:

- **Equity position risk.** Equity exposures attract specific risk and general market risk. Specific risk attracts a capital charge of 8% of all long equity positions calculated on a mark to market basis. For highly liquid and diversified portfolios this may be reduced to 4%. The capital charge for general market risk is 8% of all long equity positions on a mark to market basis.
- **Foreign Exchange risk.** Any risk of impairment of an asset due to deterioration in the exchange rate between the currency of the asset and the bank's base currency. The capital charge is 8% on the overall net position.
- **Commodities and Inventory risk.** The risk associated with holding or taking long positions in commodities. The capital charge can be calculated using a maturity ladder approach or the simplified approach. In the maturity ladder approach the capital charge is based on the sum of the net position per time band. Offsetting between time bands is permissible subject to a surcharge. Any net position after offsetting attracts a capital charge of 15%. In the simplified approach, the net position in each commodity

attracts a 15% capital charge to cater for directional risk plus an additional charge of 3% of the gross positions to cater for basis risk.

16.4.4 Operational Risk

Operational risk is defined as the risk of losses resulting from inadequate or failed internal processes, people and systems or from external events. Under the IFSB capital adequacy guidelines this not only includes legal risk, but also *sharia'a* compliance risk. In line with the Basel II Accord, operational risk excludes strategic and reputational risks.

The IFSB guidelines allow for either the Basic Indicator Approach or Standardised Approach as defined in the Basel II Accord. Under the Basic Indicator Approach, the capital charge is calculated as 15% of annual average gross income averaged over the previous three years. Under the Standardised Approach the percentage varies from 12% to 18% depending on the line of business. However, the lines of business as defined in the Basel II Accord may not be directly applicable to Islamic banks, and it is therefore suggested to apply the Basic Indicator Approach for the time being.

16.4.5 Capital Adequacy for Different Transaction Types

For each of the different transaction types outlined in section chapter 4 the capital adequacy treatment is defined by the IFSB in their capital adequacy standard. Summarised, the following treatments apply:

- *Salam* –The risk weight in a *salam* transaction is based on the counterparty or guarantor[36] rating, with unrated counterparties attracting a risk weight of 100%. The market risk on the commodity is measured separately applying a maturity ladder approach in which the capital charge is dependent on the maturity of the transaction, or by applying the simplified approach in which the capital charge equals 15% of the net position plus 3% of the gross long plus short positions. In the event a parallel *salam* is in place to cover the commodity exposure, only the 3% charge is applied to cater for any potential losses in the event the commodity can not be delivered.
- *Istisna* – The risk weight of an *istisna* transaction depends on the characteristics of the transaction. In both cases, the risk weight is initially based on the rating or the ultimate buyer.

---

[36] It is worth noting that in Islamic finance, guarantees can not be bought or sold, but only provided free of charge.

- **Full recourse *istisna* and *istisna* with parallel *istisna*.** In this case, the bank has full recourse on the buyer of the asset. If no rating is available, the transaction will attract a 100% risk weight.
- **Limited and non-recourse *istisna*.** In this case, the bank has only limited or even no recourse to the ultimate buyer. If no rating is available, the risk weight will depend on the supervisory slotting approach for specialised financing. An additional 20% risk weight may need to be added to cater for the price risk to which the underlying contract is exposed.
- *Ijara* – Under an *ijara wa iqtina* or finance lease, the risk weight is based on the rating of the lessee since the residual value risk of the underlying asset is not borne by the bank. Under an operating lease, the bank is exposed to the credit risk of the lessee for payment of the rentals and market risk for the residual value.
- *Musharaka* – The risk weight of a *musharaka* transaction depends on the intent of the underlying transaction.
  - **Private commercial enterprises with an identifiable underlying asset** (i.e. for trading activities). The investor's exposure is in first instance to the asset. In the event of default, the bank will be paid out of the proceeds of the sale of the asset. In the event the proceeds are below the original investment, the *sukuk* holder has an exposure to the counterparty for the residual. The risk weight is determined based on the market risk of the underlying asset.
  - **Private commercial enterprises to undertake a business venture.** In this type of transaction there is no identifiable underlying asset. The risk weight is based on the equity stake in the underlying venture, and as such this type of transaction is treated as an equity investment resulting in a risk weight of 400%.
  - **Joint ownership of real estate or moveable assets.** These transactions are typically structured as diminishing *musharaka*. The partnership is for a definite timescale, is not a going concern, and has an identifiable underlying asset (e.g. real estate, car). The investor's initial exposure is to the asset. In the event of default, the bank will be paid out of the sales proceeds of the asset. In the event the proceeds are below the original investment, the bank has an exposure to the counterparty for the residual. The risk weight is dependent on the counterparty rating, with unrated counterparties attracting a 100% risk weight.
- *Mudaraba* - Risk weight is based on the equity stake in the underlying asset, and as such this type of transaction is treated as an equity investment, resulting in a risk weight of 400%.

- Any risk mitigants will be taken into consideration in the determination of the risk weight.

16.4.6 Capital Adequacy for *Sukuk*

The popularity of *sukuk* warrants some specific attention regarding their capital adequacy treatment. As defined in section 4.4.2, *sukuk* are certificates of beneficial ownership rights in a pool of underlying assets, which either allow for the underlying assets to be considered as collateral (asset backed *sukuk*) or not (asset based *sukuk*). The impact of the new Basel II rules and the derived IFSB capital adequacy standards on the *sukuk* portfolio is dependent on whether they are considered to be asset backed or asset based, and in addition on how the regulator views the instrument. This will differ for regions where the IFSB standards are followed and those where these are not taken into consideration.

The current capital adequacy standard only applies to *sukuk* purchased by the financial institution, but not to *sukuk* originated, issued or serviced by the bank (i.e. securitisation exposures). Securitisation exposures are covered in a separate exposure draft[37]. The current IFSB exposure draft covers asset backed *sukuk* which are treated on a 'look-through' basis, i.e. the risk weights that apply are those of the underlying assets. The new IFSB exposure draft covers asset based *sukuk* which attract the risk weight of the obligor subject to any credit enhancement. Summarised, the following treatments apply:

16.4.6.1 *Sukuk* held as investment in the banking book
The treatment of the *sukuk* for capital adequacy purposes depends on the underlying transaction type and the counterparty rating[38]:

- *Sukuk al salam* – Until delivery and sale of the asset, the risk weight in a *sukuk al salam* is based on the counterparty or guarantor rating. Unrated counterparties attract a 100% risk weight. Market risk does not apply as it is mitigated by the inclusion of a parallel *salam* contract which is a *sharia'a* compliant hedge.
- *Sukuk al istisna* – Risk weight is based on the counterparty rating with unrated counterparties attracting a 100% risk weight. An additional 20%

---

[37] Islamic Financial Services Board (2007) *Capital Adequacy Requirements for Sukuk Securitisations and Real Estate Investments* December 2007.

[38] It should be noted that *salam, ijara,* and *musharaka sukuk* are treated using the so-called "look-through" principle which means that the exposure is to the underlying asset.

risk weight will be added to cater for the price risk to which the underlying contract is exposed.

- *Sukuk al ijara* – Under an *ijara wa iqtina* or finance lease, the risk weight is based on the rating of the lessee since the residual value risk of the underlying asset is not borne by the *sukuk* holders[39].
- *Sukuk al musharaka* – The risk weight of a *sukuk al musharaka* depends on the intent of the underlying transaction.
  - **Private commercial enterprises with an identifiable underlying asset** (i.e. for trading activities). The investor's exposure is in first instance to the asset. In the event of default, the *sukuk* holder will be paid out of the sales proceeds of the asset. In the event the proceeds are below the original investment, the *sukuk* holder has an exposure to the counterparty for the residual. The risk weight is determined based on the market risk of the underlying asset.
  - **Private commercial enterprises to undertake a business venture.** In this type of transaction there is no identifiable underlying asset. The risk weight is based on the equity stake in the underlying venture, and as such this type of *sukuk* is treated as an equity investment resulting in a risk weight of 400%.
  - **Joint ownership of real estate or moveable assets.** These transactions are typically structured as diminishing *musharaka*. The partnership is for a definite timescale, is not a going concern, and has an identifiable underlying asset (e.g. real estate, car). The investor's initial exposure is to the asset. In the event of default, the *sukuk* holder will be paid out of the sales proceeds of the asset. In the event the proceeds are below the original investment, the *sukuk* holder has an exposure to the counterparty for the residual. The risk weight is dependent on the counterparty rating, with unrated counterparties attracting a 100% risk weight.
- *Sukuk al mudaraba* - Risk weight is based on the equity stake in the underlying asset, and as such this type of *sukuk* is treated as an equity investment, resulting in a risk weight of 400%.

---

[39] Under an operating lease, the *sukuk* holders own the asset at the end of the lease, which results in added uncertainty regarding the value of the *sukuk* at maturity. This is often resolved by the presence of a purchase undertaking from the lessor to purchase the asset at a pre-agreed price. This has attracted considerable resistance from a group of scholars who take the stance that the purchase price should be the market value at time of sale. This debate is currently on-going.

Any risk mitigants will be taken into consideration in the determination of the risk weight.

16.4.6.2 *Sukuk* in the trading book.

Sukuk held in the trading book is treated similar to bond positions and attracts specific risk as well as general market risk. The provision for specific risk depends on the risk weight of the issue and the residual time to maturity as outlined in the table below.

Counterparty type	Residual Maturity	Risk Weight
Government		0.00%
Investment Grade	6 months of less	0.25%
	6 – 24 months	1.00%
	Exceeding 24 months	1.60%
Others		8%

Table 12: Risk Weight for *sukuk* in the trading book (IFSB)

The provision for general market risk depends on the residual time to maturity or to the next re-pricing date and varies on a sliding scale from 0% for residual terms of less than 1 month to 6% for residual maturities of over 20 years.

16.4.6.3 *Sukuk* origination

Sukuk originated by the bank is treated in line with the requirements for securitisation. This standard is currently still an exposure draft and is expected to be finalised by January 2009. If the ownership of the underlying asset is transferred to the holders, the Islamic financial institution may benefit from reduced capital requirements provided that criteria regarding risk transfer and control over the asset are satisfied. In the event the financial institution provides support to the issue, holds a part of the issue, or provides liquidity facilities or credit enhancements partial capital relief is possible as follows:

- Originator provides implicit support. In this case the originator must hold capital against all of the exposure associated with the securitisation position.
- Originator holds part of the issue. In this case, the originator is required to deduct any holding from capital.
- Liquidity facilities attract a risk weight of 20% for maturities lower than one year and 50% for a maturity exceeding one year. At the discretion of the supervisor, servicer cash advance facilities can be assigned 0% risk weight.
- Originator holds a small equity share in the underlying pool of securitised assets. The originators residual equity share is treated as a deduction from capital (equivalent to a risk weight of 1,250% if the CAR is 8%).

16.5 Capital Adequacy for Islamic Banks around the World

Whether or not the IFSB capital adequacy guidelines have an implication for individual banks is mainly associated with their country of incorporation, and it largely depends on the regulatory system. In those countries where Islamic banks are regulated under a separate framework the IFSB guidelines often apply in part or in full. In countries where Islamic banks are regulated under the same framework as conventional banks however, this is not necessarily the case, and the Basel II guidelines may be applied instead. Although this may result in some transaction types attracting a higher risk weight and hence a higher capital requirement than its equivalent products in conventional finance, regulators are often actively engaged with the banks – Islamic and conventional – to ensure a level playing field exists for the banks in their jurisdiction.

Malaysia and Bahrain for instance have dual banking systems and regulate conventional and Islamic banks separately. For Islamic banks, they follow the IFSB rules reasonably closely. The United Kingdom on the other hand, does not have a dual banking system and the Financial Services Authority (FSA) authorises and regulates Islamic Banks within the same framework as conventional banks. In the European Economic Community (EEC), the Basel II framework has been incorporated in the law by means of the Capital Requirements Directive (CRD) which applies to all member states. The FSA follows the CRD, and has implemented the new regulations effective 1 January 2008.

16.6 Expected Future Developments in Capital Adequacy

The IFSB has worked closely with the BCBS in the past and will continue to work with that committee to seek regulatory improvements for Islamic banks in the future. However, given that Basel II has only recently been finalised, no immediate changes to the accord's regulatory capital treatment of *mudaraba* and *musharaka* transactions are expected. The structures of *mudaraba* and *musharaka* transactions are capital intensive – and are therefore more expensive from the bank's perspective. Consequently, Islamic banks have to take the cost of capital into consideration when they are advising clients and when they are developing new transaction types in the future. In fact, one of the questions that must be addressed as part of the advisory function of an Islamic bank is whether the client's interest can be served equally well with structures separate from the *mudaraba* and *musharaka*. *Mudaraba* or *musharaka* transactions give the holder a share in the underlying asset which could potentially become impaired. The holder will have no claim against this impairment and as a result the equity treatment is justifiable. As a result, the *mudaraba* and *musharaka* transaction types and the *sukuk* based on these transaction types will be a disadvantage to clients since the additional cost of capital will be passed onto the client.

The treatment of *sukuk* on the other hand is broadly comparable to conventional bonds, due to which Islamic banks holding *sukuk* are, depending on the underlying transaction type, neither advantaged nor disadvantaged compared to bond holders. If the underlying transaction type is *mudaraba* or *musharaka* however, the equity treatment equally applies resulting in a higher capital charge. Contrary to bonds, the holder of an asset based *sukuk* is the owner of the underlying asset which behaves like collateral. However, in the majority of jurisdictions the law does not give effective recourse to the underlying assets in these transactions. Consequently, the exposure of the *sukuk* holder is to the obligor and not the asset. Asset based *sukuk* on the other hand are similar to bonds and are not collateralised in which case the holder has direct recourse to the obligor. As a result, in the majority of international jurisdictions, a level playing field is created between conventional bond holders and *sukuk* holders.

17 How to Value a Bank[40]

The requirement to measure current and future (expected) profitability and thus the ability to determine the value of a firm is not just a concept of recent years, but rather one that has evolved over the past two and a half centuries. As early as 1776, Adam Smith describes, in his epic tome known as *The Wealth of Nations*, how the owner of capital will always invest in those projects that provide a return over and above his cost of capital, and will refrain from investing in anything that does not at least meets his cost. In addition, his return should compensate for any risk he takes.

In the late 1800s, early 1900s, the ownership structure of companies started to change and management of the corporation and ownership became increasingly segregated. This, combined with the general increase in company size, resulted in a situation where the ability to provide an accurate valuation for a company became more and more important.

Although the management often owns shares in the company, the average shareholder, or owner of the capital, has only limited control over the management of the firm he invests in, especially when it comes to large companies. Beyond the Shareholder's Annual General Meeting, his control is limited to voting with his feet, i.e. if the shareholder is not convinced the company is run very well, the only choice he has is to sell his shares. Having said that, institutional investors are becoming more vocal when it comes to the company's performance and, given that their shareholding is large enough, can influence the company's direction.

The shareholders decision to invest in a share or not will largely depend on his estimate of the company value compared to the share price and it remains therefore important for any investor to be able to independently determine the value of a firm as part of his investment decision making process. The share price of a company factors in the estimation of the value of the company, as well as any expectations regarding the profitability for the period since the last results and is generally accepted as the purest market indicator of the value of the firm. However, it is subject to market sentiment and, although it is a good benchmark, the share price hardly classifies as an independent valuation.

---

[40] An earlier version of this chapter, focussing solely on the valuation of banks, has been published in the book *How to run a bank* edited by Stephen Timewell and Brain Caplen, Financial Times Business 2008.

All is not lost however. Over the past few decades, a multitude of different valuation tools have been invented and have subsequently been subject to extensive research. Some have been discarded as soon as they started to appear, but others have shown a remarkable resilience. Interestingly enough, those models that have been around for a long term seem to hold up to scrutiny best. The remainder of this chapter will identify the components that need to be considered in a good valuation model and which models are easily applicable to value a company from a third party perspective. Banks are a special class of companies and are generally excluded when valuing companies and the possibility to apply a valuation model to them is reviewed at the end of this chapter.

17.1 The Components

Any model that is used as a tool for company valuation will have to incorporate returns, capital and cost of capital. Interlinked with these three components are sustainable growth and risk. Each of these components is described in further detail below.

17.1.1 Growth

In order for expected future growth to have any impact on the valuation of a firm, it needs to be sustainable over prolonged periods of time. The sustainable growth rate is generally measured by multiplying the proportion of income the firm retains for reinvestment by the return on equity. The underlying assumptions are:

1. **Speed of growth.** A firm is managed in order to grow as fast as possible;

2. **Capital levels.** There is no requirement to issue new equity, in order to sustain growth; and

3. **Capital structure.** Growth can be sustained while maintain the current capital structure and dividend policies.

17.1.2 Risk

Running a business is associated with taking a view on a particular development in the market or an industry and is inherently incorporating a risk in some shape or form. Unfortunately, there is no such thing as a company that does not run any risk at all, and an equity investment could result in total loss of the capital provided. Investors are only interested in higher risk assets if they fit within their risk profile, although the fact that the return needs to reflect the additional risk they are taking is of equal importance.

17.1.3 Returns

Based on the generally accepted notion that a company's value is closely linked to the net present value of the potential cash distributions it is expected to generate, earnings are the most logical measure of return. Earnings have their own limitations as a result of the application of realisation and matching principles in accounting, which result in recognition of earnings in different periods than the receipt or disbursement of the underlying cash flows. However, even after taking these limitations into account, current earnings still provide the strongest indication of the profitability of a firm. Future earnings estimates need to incorporate micro-economics of the firm as well as competitive interaction of the firm with firms in the same industry.

17.1.4 Capital and its Cost

The capital of a firm consists of equity capital and, where applicable, long- and short-term debt. The cost of capital is one of the most critical parts of any valuation model, and represents the opportunity cost of the investment in the firm's existing assets. The cost of capital needs to reflect the perceived risk of the firm.

Differences in risk levels and the potential availability of collateral result in a situation where equity and debt require a different return. Lower risk debt logically attracts a lower return then higher risk debt which in turn attracts a lower return than equity. For valuation purposes, the Weighted Average Cost of Capital (WACC) is generally applied to provide a reasonably accurate approximation to determine the total cost of capital of a firm.

17.2 The Models

The two main streams of valuation models most commonly used by analysts are Residual Income models and Discounted Cash Flow (DCF) models, each with their own advantages and disadvantages. DCF models determine the value of a company as the present value of all expected future cash distributions discounted at the opportunity cost of capital. They do not, however, incorporate any upside the company may have generated by re-investing part of its profits back into the company, which may provide an even higher return going forward.

Residual Income models calculate the value of a firm at a certain point in time as the book value of capital at that point in time plus the expected future earnings over and above the cost of capital for the indefinite future. However, given the competitive nature of most markets, any excess earnings have a tendency to revert to the mean over a period of three years and do not need to be forecast beyond this period. Instead, they can be substituted by a continuing value for the going concern which makes the model infinitely more useful from a practical perspective. Residual Income models have been around for a long time and have certainly proven their worth when it comes to general accuracy and reliability of results. In addition, these models can be applied using publicly available accounting data and do not require too many assumptions, which make them highly acceptable for practical application.

Does It Work?

The proof, as the saying goes, is in the pudding. How accurate is the model in determining the value? Given an efficient market where all publicly available information and future expectations are reflected in the share price and assuming rational investor behaviour, it would be safe to state that the resulting value from the Residual Income model divided by the number of shares should be the same as the current share price, or at least within an acceptable variation. Frankel and Lee[41] have executed extensive testing on a large population of firms to prove this and have found that the Residual Income model does, within reasonable limits, provide a very accurate result. They have, however, specifically excluded financial institutions from their research.

17.3 The Special Case of Banks

What is so special about banks that makes most researchers run a mile, and why do they remain inherently difficult to value? For starters, banks run additional risks such as liquidity and settlement risk, which do not exist in other firms. In addition, banks have the funds of depositors at their disposal that are applied to their day to day operations. Even though this results in the situation where clients are major liability holders, these funds are not considered to be part of the capital base of a bank, and should rather be viewed as a key source to fund loan and investment operations. Hence, for valuation purposes, only equity capital and reserves should be taken into consideration as capital when valuing a bank. In addition, the risks a bank runs are different in nature from other organisations.

Although all these issues make banks more difficult to value, research[42] has proven that, given the right application of the components, the Residual

---

[41] Frankel, R and M.C. Lee (1998)   *Accounting Valuation, Market Expectation, and Cross-sectional Stock Returns,* Journal of Accounting and Economics, 25, 283 – 319
[42] Schoon, Natalie; *Residual Income Models and the Valuation of Conventional and Islamic Banks;* University of Surrey (2005)

Income model produces a reasonably accurate value compared to the market price for banks as well as for other types of organisations. So, perhaps banks are not really that different when it comes to valuing them.

17.4 The Special Case of Islamic Banks

Islamic banks generally have similar issues to the ones outlined for conventional banks, and it should therefore, in principle, be possible to value them using the same model. However, due to the limited availability (or in some cases complete absence) of information required, such as the market and risk-free rates of return, as well as analyst consensus forecast data for Islamic banks, some of the elements of the residual income model need to be substituted by estimations. The issues associated with the valuation of Islamic banks can be summarised as follows:

- **Market efficiency.** Islamic banks operate in markets that are, at best, weak-form efficient, and where the market rate of return is less reliable;
- **Market prices.** For Islamic banks listed on a stock exchange, the prices are not considered to provide an accurate representation of the value, and the market is highly illiquid;
- **Data availability.** Islamic banks are generally not listed on a stock exchange and are not necessarily required to publish their annual reports;
- **Definition of capital.** Unrestricted investment accounts have characteristics of share capital and should on that basis be included in capital. On the other hand, they typically have stable returns and capital is informally guaranteed which would imply they should be treated as deposits in conventional banks;
- **Lunar or solar calendar.** The length of the financial year may differ where the financial year is based on the lunar calendar (see page 2).

The same research has shown that with careful estimation of the values, it is possible to value Islamic banks by applying the residual model and to compare the valuation of Islamic banks with those of conventional banks.

17.5 Can a Bank be Valued?

The Residual Income model may be old fashioned and while it may not have a lot of bells and whistles, it is both in practice and in theory the most widely used and tested model to determine the value of any firm. It applies publicly available data, is easy to use, has a good degree of accuracy and can be applied to any industry. Using the right methodology to estimate growth, risk and return with a reasonable degree of accuracy over a period of approximately three years, combined with a continuing value for the going concern, the

Residual Income model can not only provide a reasonable estimate of the value of a firm, but can equally be applied to banks.

18 The Future

The principles underlying of Islamic finance such as profit and loss sharing, justness in exchange, transparency and the prohibition of usury go back a long time, and are not just associated with Islamic finance. Early philosophers have debated the same issues and during the 19th century, the United Kingdom implemented an anti-usury law for a while. Islamic finance has remarkable similarities with what is known as merchant banking, a way of doing business that has for a while been seen as old fashioned and conservative. Given the 2007 and 2008 market turmoil, banks may well have to reconsider their approach to lending and take some of the more old fashioned principles such as "do not lend to those who can not afford the payment" into consideration again.

Faith-based banking is not a new phenomenon, but rather one that has been around for a long time. Every religion has an impact on society, and many religious beliefs have found themselves incorporated in the banking system for at least some time during the history of finance. In addition, it does not just appeal to those of a particular religion either. The application of principles of fairness and justness are attractive to a large and diverse investor and depositor base, regardless of their religion. On the other hand, faith-based banks are typically small compared to their conventional counterparts, with only a fraction of the balance sheet size. Although the interest in faith-based and socially responsible investing exists, it is expected to remain a subset within the conventional mainstream financial markets.

Islamic Finance is undoubtedly experiencing remarkable growth in Muslim countries and is attracting increasingly significant interest in the West. At this point in time, the UK's Financial Services Authority has licensed five Islamic banks, one investment company and one insurance company, and interest in Islamic financial solutions is generally high.

Over the past few years the UK Government has made amendments to tax legislation in successive Finance Acts to allow for Islamic Finance products to be treated in a similar fashion for tax purposes as conventional products. However, some issues still exist such as double Stamp Duty Land Tax for properties that are subject to *sukuk*. In the 2008 Budget, it was announced that further measures to avoid double taxation for alternative investments will be taken in the 2009 Finance Act, which will open up opportunities for banks and corporates to issue *sukuk* in the UK.

At present, however, there are no marketable, liquid instruments available to Islamic financial institutions, which puts them at a disadvantage in comparison to the Islamic windows of conventional banks when it comes to accessing and managing liquidity in the market at any time and particularly at times of market stress. This is where the issue of a UK Government *sukuk* will have a major positive impact on the global Islamic financial market.

In short, while knowledge is improving and coverage is increasing there is still much to do with regard to tax and regulation before Islamic Finance becomes more comparable to conventional finance in terms of scope and depth.

Although the Islamic finance transactions all have exotic names and they take *sharia'a* principles into consideration, their underlying structures are not a million miles away from conventional banking structures. When applying the different structures to modern finance however, it needs to be ensured that any transaction is compliant with *sharia'a* and is associated with an underlying asset.

The Islamic financial market is relatively young and growing at an incredible pace which is, at least in part, to do with the large inflows of money into the Middle Eastern countries. Not only do they have funds available for investment, they also heavily invest in infrastructure and other projects in their economies.

The risks Islamic banks face are, although partly different, in many respects similar to conventional financial institutions. As long as Islamic banks are largely incorporated in emerging markets, their risk levels are likely to be higher than the overall conventional financial industry. Increasing sophistication and incorporation of banks in developed jurisdictions is likely to lead to a situation where the risk levels of Islamic and conventional banks are roughly similar.

With around 15 – 20% year on year growth over the past decades, and a similar estimated growth rate for the coming years, it is clear that the Islamic financial industry, or at least the principles it represents, is here to stay. However, although growing, the Islamic financial industry still has a way to go. The banks are relatively young and most have not gone through a full economic cycle yet. *Sharia'a* compliance differs per country and can even differ between banks. Work has started on standardisation, and although still a way off, it will eventually result in a more efficient industry, and a more level playing field. In addition, standardisation will lead to a reduced cost base across the industry. The demand for Islamic financial products does not just come from Muslims. The underlying principles attract a wide range of investors and parties looking for financing. The pricing, however, will need to be competitive in order to ensure continuing demand.

Demand is increasing, but so is the supply which results in a more competitive environment. Islamic banks are not only competing with each other, but also with conventional banks and their Islamic windows and subsidiaries. Equally important, an improved regulatory environment will assist the banks operating in the Islamic financial industry achieve stability and not only the chance to get through the current rocky economical environment, but also to achieve a long-term sustainable Islamic financial industry which co exists alongside the conventional financial industry.

Appendix A – Definitions

Unlike the specific definitions provided in the relevant chapters, this appendix provides an overview of all Arabic definitions accompanied by a brief description. Additional definitions not necessarily included in the text can also be found in this list.

Word	Description
A'qd	Contract or transaction that is executed between two or more parties for mutual benefit.
Arbun	Down payment on a sales contract in which the buyer has not paid the full price or taken possession of the goods. Deposit is non-refundable. Buyer can opt to cancel the contract.
Fatwa	Declaration in Islam provided by an Islamic legal specialist.
Fiqh	Understanding of the (Islamic) Law
Fiqh Al Muamalat	Islamic commercial jurisprudence
Gharar	To deceive, cheat, delude, lure, entice and overall uncertainty. Also defined as "gharar is whose consequences are hidden" or "the sale of probable items whose existence or characteristics are not certain".
Hadith	Narrative record of the sayings and actions of the Prophet.
Halal	Permitted
Haram	Prohibited
Hawala	Transfer of money from one person to another. Recipient may charge admin charges which should not be proportionate to the sum of money.
Ijara	Bilateral contract allowing the sale of the usufruct for a specified rent and a specified period. A lease.
Ijara wa Iqtina	Lease with transfer of ownership at the end of the lease period or finance lease. Variations exist such as the *ijara muntahia bittamleek* which is a finance lease structure in which the lessee has the option to exercise his right to purchase the asset at any time during the lease period.
Istisna	Sale with deferred delivery. Payment can be in a lump sum in advance or progressively in accordance with progress made. Delivery of good is deferred.

Word	Description
Kafala	Guarantee or third party obligation
Muamalat	Activities not explicitly governed by *sharia'a* with respect to worship.
Mudaraba	Partnership contract. Sub-set of Musharaka
Mudarib	Party in a contract providing knowledge and skill
Murabaha	Deferred payment sale or instalment credit sale
Musharaka	Partnership contract.
Parallel salam	Parallel contract to an existing *salam* contract to hedge the *salam* position. Often outright sale (with deferred delivery), but could be arranged with payment at a later date using an LC or guarantee to secure the payment.
Qard	Loan
Qard al Hassan	Interest free loan. Often used in charitable context. Recipient has the moral obligation to repay the principal.
Quran	Book of God
Rab al Mal	Party in a contract providing finances
Rahn	Collateral pledged
Re-Takaful	Islamic re-insurance undertaken to reduce excessive concentration risks.
Riba	Interest
Riba al fadl	Excess compensation without any consideration (e.g. Monies passing between the parties) resulting from an exchange of sale of goods.
Riba al naseeyah	Excess resulting from predetermined interest which a lender receives over and above the principal amount it has lent out. Primary form of riba. It is the addition of a premium paid to the lender in return for waiting for his money. (Time value of Money)
Sadaqat	Voluntary charitable contribution, guided by the goodwill of the donor.
Salam	Sale with deferred delivery. Payment is paid in full and up front, delivery of good is deferred.
Sarf	Purchase and sale of currency. Only allowed at spot for equal value.
Sharia'a	Ethical framework of Islam, often referred to as Islamic Law.

Word	Description
Sukuk	Plural of Sakk. Represents partial ownership in assets. Sukuk are technically neither shares nor bonds but has characteristics of both. Profit is based on the performance of the underlying assets or projects.
Sunnah	Words or acts of the prophet
Tabarru'	Non-commercial donation or gift. Any benefit that is given by a person to another without getting anything in exchange.
Takaful	Islamic insurance comparable to mutual insurance
Tawarruq	Purchase of a commodity that is immediately sold on to a 3rd party (usually using the original seller as agent) on spot for cash. Form or reverse Murabaha.
Wa'd	Unilateral Promise. Undertaking or promise by one party to do or not do something in the future.
Wakala	Agency contract. Often applied to brokerage, asset management and investment activities.
Wakil	Agent in a Wakala or agency contract.
Zakat	Obligatory donation to charity for those who can afford it.

Selected Bibliography

Archer, S., and R.A.A. Karim (2006), *On Capital Structure, Risk Sharing and Capital Adequacy in Islamic Banks,* International Journal of Theoretical and Applied Finance, Vol. 9, No. 3 (2006) 269-280.

Archer, Simon (Editor), Rifaat Abdel Karim (Editor)(2007), *Islamic Finance: The Regulatory Challenge*, J. Wiley and Sons

Copeland, T.E, T. Koller and J. Murrin (2005), *Valuation: Measuring and Managing the Value of Companies*, 4th Edition, New York: John Wiley & Sons

Brealey, R.A., S.C. Myers, and A.J. Marcus (2003), *Fundamentals of Corporate Finance,* New York: McGraw-Hill

Davies, Glyn (2002), *A history of money from ancient times to the present day,* 3rd ed. Cardiff, University of Wales Press

DiVanna, Joseph A (2006), *Understanding Islamic Banking: The Value Proposition That Transcends Cultures*, Leonardo and Francis Press

Frankel, R and M.C. Lee (1998), *Accounting Valuation, Market Expectation, and Cross-sectional Stock Returns,* Journal of Accounting and Economics, 25, 283 – 319

Goff, Jacques Le (1990)m *Your Money or Your Life,. Economy and Religion in the Middle Ages*, Zone Books

Goldshmidt, Arthur (2001), *A Concise History of the Middle East*, 7th edition, Westview Press

Iqbal, Munawar and Philip Moyneux (2005), *Thirty Years of Islamic Banking – History, Performance and Prospects*, Palgrave Macmillan

Iqbal, Zamir and Abbas Mirakhor (2007), *An Introduction to Islamic Finance, Theory and Practice*, Wiley Finance, 2007

Jones, Norman (1989), *God and The Moneylenders,* Blackwell

Kohn, Meir (1999), *The Origins of Western Economic Success: Commerce, Finance, and Government in Preindustrial Europe;* http://www.dartmouth.edu/~mkohn/orgins.html. Unpublished

MacMillan C, and R. Stone (2004) *Elements of the Law of Contract*, University of London – The External Programme

Monroe, A.E. – Editor (1948), *Early Economic Thought, selections from Economic Literature prior to Adam Smith*, Cambridge, Harvard University Press

BIBLIOGRAPHY

Parkin, Michael (2007), *Economics*, 8th edition, Pearson Addison Wesley

Smith, Adam (1776), *An Inquiry into the Nature and Causes of the Wealth of Nations*. Complete and Unabridged version, The Modern Library Classics, 2000

The History of Economic Thought Website
http://cepa.newschool.edu/het/home.htm

http://www.londonexternal.ac.uk/current_students/programme_resources/laws/subject_guides/law_contract/law_of_con_chs1to4.pdf

Index